故宮玉器選萃

Masterworks of Chinese Jade
in the National Palace Museum

國立故宮博物院印行

Published by the National Palace Museum
Taipei, Taiwan, Republic of China

序

　　三代遺物，存於今者，彝器之外，莫重於玉瑞。然古玉之著錄，在宋僅有呂大臨之考古圖，龍大淵之古玉圖譜，在元則朱德潤之古玉圖。而呂氏朱氏之作，所錄玉瑞，為數極微，龍氏之作，顯然偽書，均不足以詁經證史。迨清道光中，瞿中溶氏始為古玉圖錄，其後吳大澂氏又為古玉圖考，於是論玉圖籍，始見增多，而人知古玉與吉金同尊，非徒供玩賞而已也。

　　故宮所藏玉器之富，為世界公私收藏所不及，其中古代遺物，有裨經義者固多，其近代雕琢，鏤刻精巧者，尤不可勝數，念自文物遷臺以來，對於玉瑞一項，尚無專輯，常思集印，以廣流傳。

　　本輯所選，自三代以迄於清，新舊玉器，都凡五十件，念玉瑞之可貴，固在其形制，足資徵古，而其色澤之溫潤，比德君子，尤足珍貴，因用彩色精印，以存其真。

　　此冊之選件與編輯，悉由本院那志良處長、吳鳳培編輯及陳瑠美技佐共同擔任，工作多日，始獲完成，特附識之，以不沒其辛勤也。

　　　　　　　　　　　中華民國五十八年十二月十五日　　蔣復璁敬識

序

　今日に残る三代（夏、商、周）の遺物のうち、彝器（宗廟にそなえる祭祀用の銅器）をのぞいては玉が最も重んぜられている。しかし、古玉の記録としては、宋時代に呂大臨の「考古図」と龍大淵の「古玉図譜」、元時代に朱徳潤の「古玉図」があるだけである。だが呂氏、朱氏の著作は、収録した玉の数が極めて少なく、龍氏の著作は明らかに偽作であって、いずれも資料として用いるわけにはいかないものである。

　清時代の道光年間になって、瞿中溶氏がはじめて「古玉図譜」を著わし、そののち呉大澂氏もまた「古玉図攷」を著わした。こうして、玉研究に関する図書がようやく多くなり、人々も古玉を吉金（彝鼎）と同様に尊重しはじめ、ただ単に玩賞するだけではなくなったのである。

　故宮所蔵の玉器の豊富なことは、世界の公私蔵の玉器の及ぶところではない。殊に古代の遺物には経義を補益するものが多く、近代の彫琢を施した玉には、彫刻の精巧なものが数しれない。文物が台湾へ移って以来、これら玉器についてはまだ専門の書を刊行していないので、これを編集出版して世に広めたいものと、つねづね考えていたのである。

　この選萃に選んだのは、三代から清に至るまでの、新旧の玉器、全五十点である。玉の価値は、その形態や製作方法が古い時代をうかがい知るよすがになるばかりでなく、君子の徳にもたとえるべきその温潤な色沢が、殊に珍重されるのである。その意味で、この選萃では、玉のまことの姿を精巧な原色印刷によって再現してある。

　作品選定と編集にあたっては、本院の那志良処長、呉鳳培編輯および陳瑠美技佐が共同担当し、多日にわたって業務に従い、これを完成した。特に付記して、その労をねぎらうものである。

1969年12月15日　蔣復璁敬識

Preface

Aside from sacrificial vessels, propitious objects of jade occupy the position of chief importance among those objects left to us from the period of the Three Ancient Dynasties, that is, the Hsia, Shang, and Chou dynasties. Nevertheless, old writings and catalogues on jade are limited to Lü Ta-lin's *K'ao-ku-t'u* and Lung Ta-yüan's *Ku-yü-t'u-p'u* from the Sung dynasty, while from the Yüan dynasty we have Chu Te-jun's *Ku-yü-t'u*. The objects of jade recorded in the works by Chu and Lü are however infinitesimally small in number; and the work by Lung, being an obvious forgery, is totally unsatisfactory for use in authentification or explanation of jade objects. Ch'ü Chung-jung first came out with his *Ku-yü-t'u-lu* in the Tao-kuang era (1821–1850) of the Ch'ing dynasty, and afterwards Wu Ta-ch'eng wrote the *Ku-yü-t'u-k'ao*. Thereafter, illustrated writings discussing ancient jade began to experience a marked increase, and people realized that ancient jade shared the same esteem as ancient bronzes and that it was not merely something to provide amusement and enjoyment.

The richness of the National Palace Museum's collection of jade objects and utensils is unmatched by that of any other collection, public or private, in the world. Among its objects from the period of the Three Ancient Dynasties, those that are of benefit in understanding the meaning of the Classics are quite numerous, while its examples of carving and polishing in jade from more recent periods, fine examples of brilliant skill in the lapidary arts, are especially plentiful, indeed, almost uncountable.

Recalling that we have not yet prepared a publication exclusively devoted to so much as a single item of jade ever since our cultural treasures were shifted to Taiwan, we have often thought to gather materials together for publication in order to disseminate them widely for the benefit of general knowledge and those particularly interested in the subject. Altogether fifty pieces of both ancient jade and jade from more recent dynasties, extending from the period of the Three Ancient Dynasties to the Ch'ing dynasty, have been selected for the present publication. If one recalls wherein jade has been highly valued, it is that the fashioning of its forms are sufficient to reveal its antique flavour in full measure, while the warm sheen of its lustrous finish, oft compared to the virtuous gentleman of superior bearing, is quite enough to make it highly prized. We have therefore used colour to print this volume in order to remain faithful to the true spirit of the original pieces.

Responsibility for selecting the objects and compiling and editing the materials presented in this album rests jointly with Na Chih-liang, Curator, Wu Feng-p'ei, Editor, and Ch'en Liu-mei, Technical Assistant. Not wishing to leave buried in obscurity the good efforts of these people who have worked so hard on this volume, I have taken the occasion of the completion of the work to make special recognition of it here.

Chiang Fu-tsung
December 15, 1969
Taipei, Republic of China

圖版目錄

Content of Plates

右：周　舊玉戚　部份

right: Ch'i, Archaic Jade Axe, detail

1　商　舊玉鳥紋珮
Pei, Archaic Jade Pendent, Shang dynasty (1766–1122 B.C.)

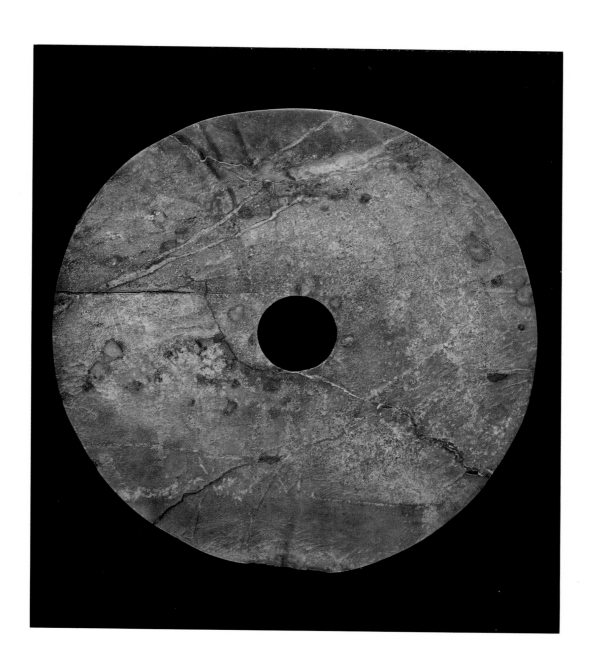

2　商　舊玉素璧

Pi, Archaic Jade Plain Disc,　Shang dynasty (1766–1122 B.C.)

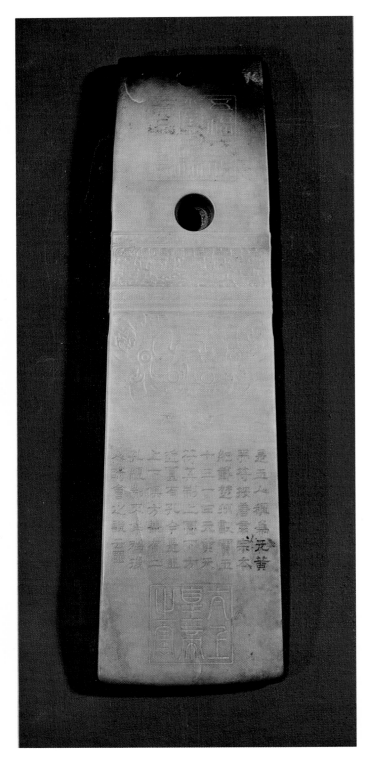

3 商　舊玉圭

Kuei, Archaic Jade Tablet,　Shang dynasty

(1766–1122 B.C.)

4 周　舊玉圭

Kuei, Archaic Jade Tablet,　Chou dynasty

(1122–221 B.C.)

5　周　舊玉穀紋璧

Pi, Archaic Jade Disc,　Chou dynasty (1122–221 B.C.)

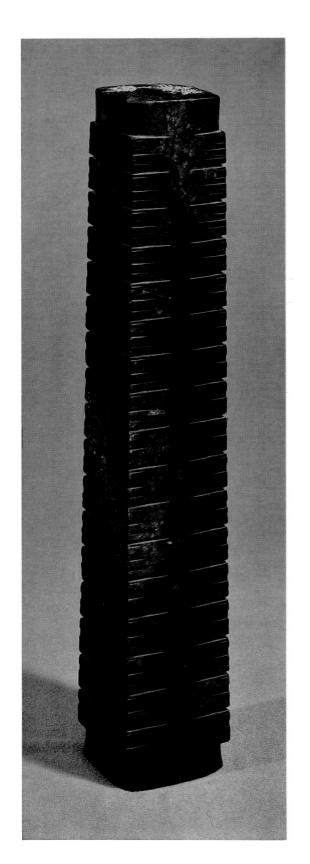

6　周　舊玉琮
Ts'ung, Archaic Jade Tube,　Chou dynasty
(1122–221 B.C.)

7　周　舊玉琮
Ts'ung, Archaic Jade Tube,　Chou dynasty (1122–221 B.C.)

8 周 舊玉璜

Huang, Archaic Jade, Chou dynasty (1122–221 B.C.)

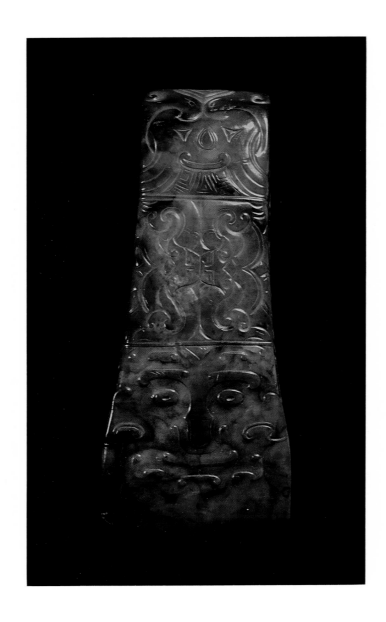

9 周　舊玉斧
Fu, Archaic Jade Axe,　Chou dynasty (1122–221 B.C.)

10　周　舊玉戚

Ch'i, Archaic Jade Axe,　Chou dynasty (1122–221 B.C.)

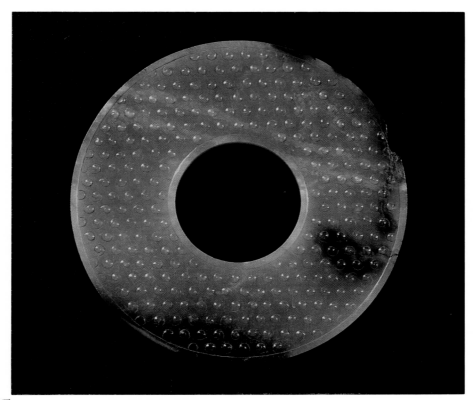

11　周　舊玉穀紋環
Huan, Archaic Jade Disc,　Chou dynasty (1122–221 B.C.)

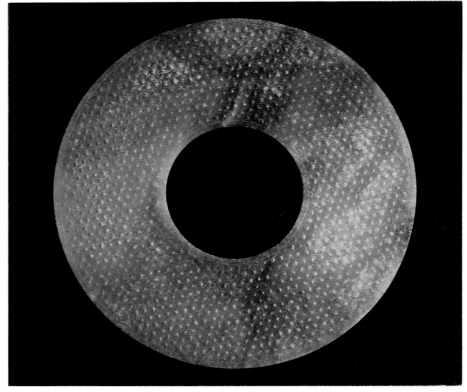

12　周　舊玉環
Huan, Archaic Jade Disc,　Chou dynasty (1122–221 B.C.)

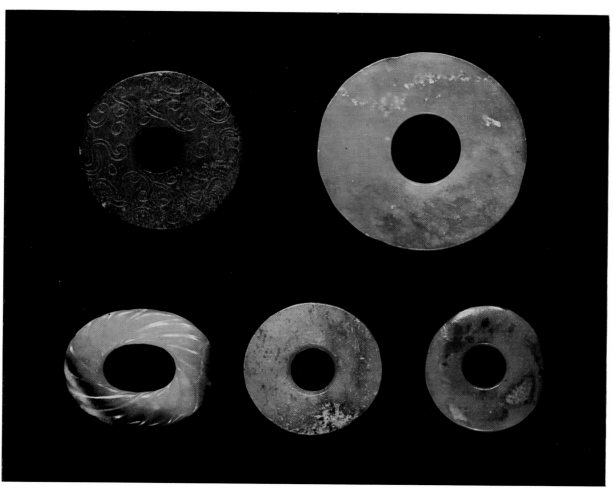

13 戰國 舊玉系璧 五件
Pi, Archaic Jade Discs (5 pieces), Warring States period (481–221 B.C.)

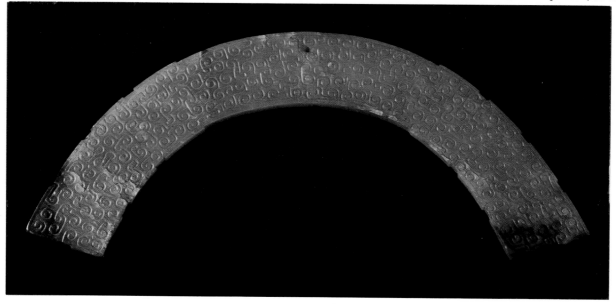

14 戰國 舊玉珩
Heng, Archaic Jade Girdle Ornament, Warring states period. (481–221 B.C.)

15 漢 舊玉蠶紋璧
Pi, Archaic Jade Disc, Han dynasty (206 B.C.–220 A.D.)

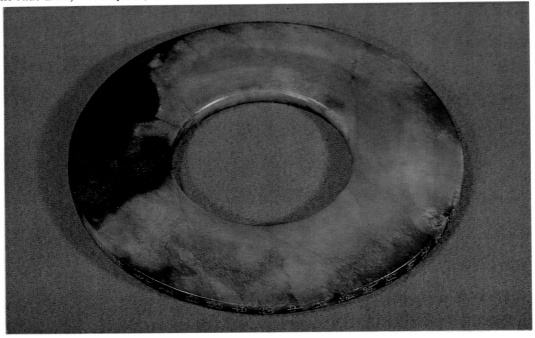

16 漢 舊玉蟬紋瑗
Yuan, Archaic Jade Disc, Han dynasty (206 B.C.–220 A.D.)

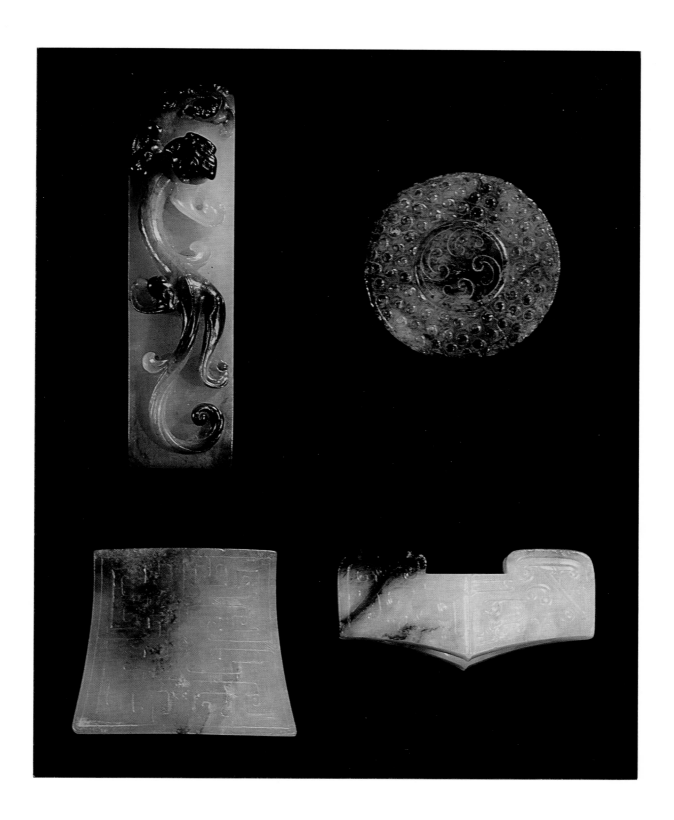

17　漢　舊玉琫・璏・璲・珌

Peng, Wei, Shui, Pi,　Archaic Jade Sword Ornaments,　Han dynasty (206 B.C.–220 A.D.)

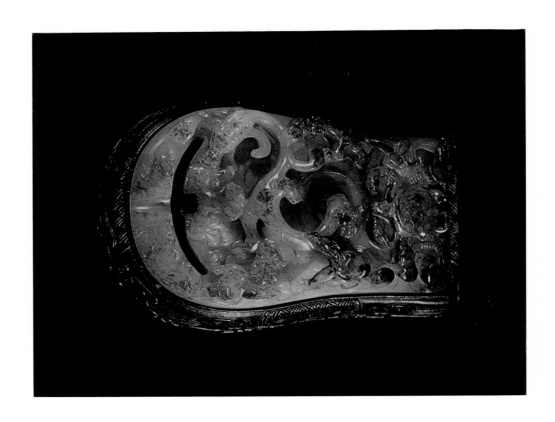

18　漢　舊玉帶頭

Tai t'ou, Archaic Jade Belt Ring,　Han dynasty (206 B.C.–220 A.D.)

19 漢 舊玉哈蟬 八件

Han, Archaic Jade Cicada (8 pieces), Han dynasty (206 B.C.–220 A.D.)

20 漢 舊玉辟邪

Pi hsieh, Archaic Jade Winged Beast, Han dynasty (206 B.C.–220 A.D.)

21 漢 墨玉牧羝器架

Black Jade Brush Rest, Han dynasty (206 B.C.–220 A.D.)

22 宋 舊玉單把柸

Handled Cup, Archaic Jade, Sung dynasty (960-1279)

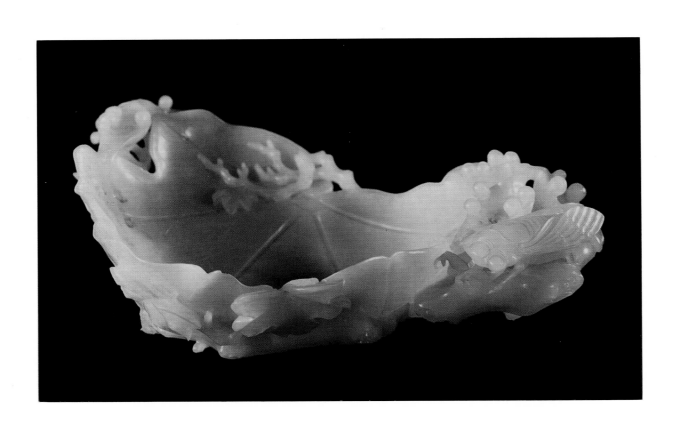

24   明　白玉秋蟬桐葉洗

Hsi, White Jade Brush Washer,　Ming dynasty (1368-1644)

25　明　白玉鰲魚花挿

Hua cha, White Jade Flower Holder,　Ming dynasty (1368–1644)

26 清 白玉茶壺
Cha hu, White Jade Teapot, Ch'ing dynasty (1644-1911)

27 清 白玉四耳彝爐

Lu, White Jade Incense Burner, Ch'ing dynasty (1644–1911)

28　清　白玉花薰
Hua hsün, White Jade Flower Perfumer,　Ch'ing dynasty (1644-1911)

29 清 白玉瑞獸尊
Tsung, White Jade Wine Vessel, Ch'ing dynasty (1644–1911)

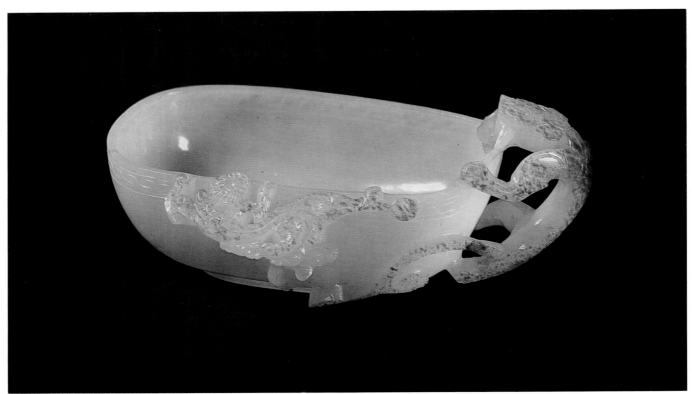

30 清 白玉螭耳栖
Pei, White Jade Cup, Ch'ing dynasty (1644–1911)

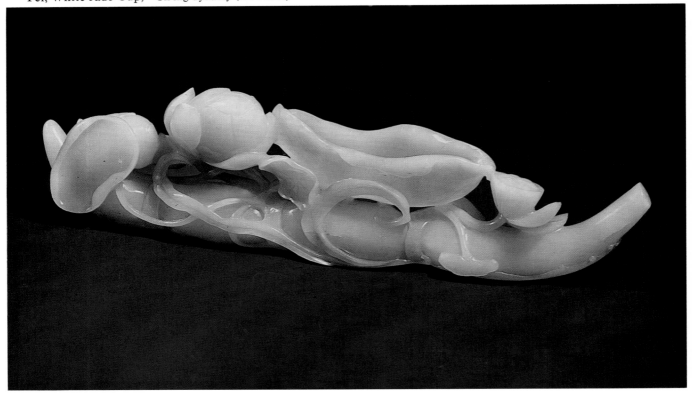

31 清 青玉蓮藕洗
Hsi, Green Jade Washer, Ch'ing dynasty (1644–1911)

32 清 白玉錦荔枝

White Jade Leechee, Ch'ing dynasty (1644-1911)

33 清 青玉爐
Lu, Green Jade Incense Burner, Ch'ing dynasty (1644-1911)

34 清 碧玉雙耳活環菊瓣洗
Hsi, Dark Green Jade Brush Washer, Ch'ing dynasty (1644-1911)

35　清　青玉天雞蓋尊

Tsung, Green Jade Covered Vase,　Ch'ing dynasty (1644–1911)

36　清　碧玉琱秋山獵騎圖筆筒

Pi tun, Dark Green Jade Brush Holder, Ch'ing dynasty (1644–1911)

37　清　碧玉璃龍三足鼎

Ting, Dark Green Jade Cauldron, Ch'ing dynasty (1644–1911)

38 清　碧玉鰲魚花揷
Hua Ch'a, Dark Green Jade Flower Holder,　Ch'ing dynasty (1644–1911)

39　清　碧玉尊

Tsung, Dark Green Jade Wine Vessel,　Ch'ing dynasty (1644–1911)

40　清　碧玉鏤空雲龍大香筒

Dark Green Jade Tube,　Ch'ing dynasty (1644–1911)

41　清　碧玉蟠龍洗

Hsi, Dark Green Jade Brush Washer,　Ch'ing dynasty (1644-1911)

42　清　碧玉琱花龍耳爐
Lu, Dark Green Jade Incense Burner,　Ch'ing dynasty (1644–1911)

43　清　黃玉連環鈕印
Yin, Yellow Jade Seals,　Ch'ing dynasty (1644–1911)

44　清　翠玉松鶴山子
Jadeite Trinket,　Ch'ing dynasty (1644–1911)

45　淸　翠玉白菜

Jadeite Cabbage,　Ch'ing dynasty (1644–1911)

46　清　翠玉松鶴挿屏

Jadeite Screen, Ch'ing dynasty (1644–1911)

47 清 紅瑪瑙蟠桃洗
Agate Brush Washer, Ch'ing dynasty (1644–1911)

48 清 瑪瑙磨具
Agate Millstone, Ch'ing dynasty (1644–1911)

49 清 墨晶筆筒
Black Crystal Brush Holder, Ch'ing dynasty (1644–1911)

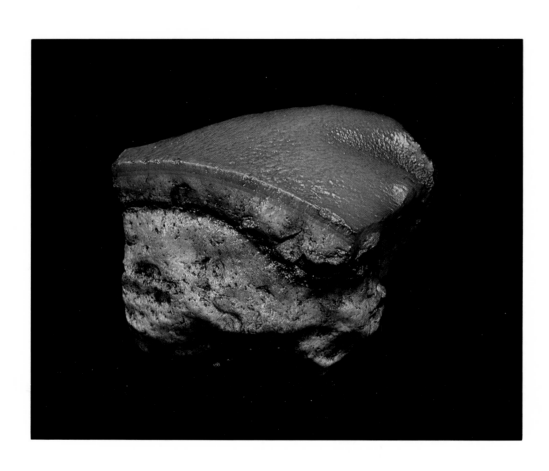

50　清　肉形石

Meat-shaped Stone, Ch'ing dynasty (1644–1911)

解說
COMMENTARY

玉　器

玉，是石的一種，有半透明體，溫潤而光澤，所以說文解字解釋「玉」字，說是「石之美者」。其實美麗的石，不僅是玉，像紅寶石、藍寶石、綠松石、青金石、碧么、瑪瑙、水晶……等，大都美麗光澤，這是古人對於玉的一種廣義說法，把所有美麗的石，統稱之爲玉。按照礦物學上所說的玉，則是分爲兩類，一類是軟玉，就是我們經常所見的白玉、青玉、黃玉、碧玉、墨玉……等；一類是硬玉，是我們經常所熟悉的翡翠。

玉的硬度是很高的，琢磨成器，不是很容易的事，我國琢玉工作，數千年來，一直是用着一種很簡單的工具，而能製造出各種不同形式的精美器物。這是中國琢玉工藝，在世界上佔很重要地位的原因之一。

玉的出產地點，古書的記載很多，但是包括了所有的美麗的石，就是前面所說的「廣義的玉」。礦物學上所稱的玉，在中國是出產在新疆和雲南兩省境內，軟玉出產在新疆，硬玉出產在雲南。

玉器的製法，是由石器的製法中演變而來，自從銅器被人知道使用以後，石器便由實用的領域中退出來。古人爲了紀念這些曾給人類造福的石器，不忍丟掉它，而變成人們崇拜的對象，敬之如神，並且用玉仿製它的形制，以垂於久遠。聰明的統治者，更利用人民這種心理，根據石斧、石鐮的形式，製定爲朝廷之禮器。

用玉製造的器物，不外三種：一種是用作紀念性的禮拜的對象，一種是朝廷所用的禮器，一種則是民間的裝飾器、喪葬器……等。人類在生活上，是不斷的求新、求進步，製造的器物，既不是爲了實用，而是一種藝術的作品，自然要耗費時間人力求其精美，因此，玉器的製作技術漸漸地，達到了美好的境域。傳世古代的器物，其琢磨之精細，使我們歎爲觀止，而這種製作技術，歷數千年而不衰。

禮器：用玉製做的，重要的是「六瑞」與「六器」。

六瑞，是政府規定不同尺度的圭與璧，發給國內最高爵位的人執掌，做爲代表他們權力的象徵。鎮圭、桓圭、信圭、躬圭，分由天子與公爵、侯爵、伯爵所執掌，其形制相同，而以尺寸長短別尊卑。穀璧、蒲璧，分由子爵、男爵所執掌，也是形制相同，而以紋

飾爲別。

六器，就是天子用以禮告天地四方的祭祀器。蒼璧、黃琮，用以禮天地；青圭、赤璋、白琥、玄璜，用以禮告東、南、西、北的四方。 這些名稱的第一字， 是代表玉的顏色， 第二字則是器的名稱。例如蒼璧，就是用蒼色玉製造的「璧」，蒼是代表天的顏色，所謂：「蒼蒼者天」，這句話是我們經常所聽到的。關於黃琮，是因爲土的色澤是黃色，所以用黃色玉製造。我國素有「天圓地方」之語，所以用圓的璧禮天，方形的琮禮地，其他四方所取之形，是根據五形之說，加以圖案化的。

符節器，是王命下達用的信符，凡遇凶荒危亂，天子就派官員持符節去傳達王命，例如珍圭、琬圭、琬圭、穀圭等，都屬於符節之器，各有其規定的使命。不外是征伐不法，褒獎善行，調解紛爭等；牙璋，則是發兵專用的符節。上古人民純樸，可以用這種形制簡單的符節，但是此類玉符容易僞造。東周以後就改用虎符，把整體的虎形，剖分爲二片，政府與將領各執其一，徵調之時，受命者把二片相合爲一，纔相信這是眞正的命令。

佩飾玉是佩帶的飾物，戴在頭上、頸間、腰間的裝飾品。人們的飾物，起初是用獸牙，鳥骨之類，經過長時期的使用，後來改用玉仿製，如玉觿、圓瑂，其形狀卽近似獸牙與骨管。其他如玉笄、玉珩、系璧、鳥獸紋珮，均爲佩玉；翁仲、剛卯也是佩玉，同時它們又是一種壓勝之物。古人有將數玉穿連成串，佩帶腰間，走起路來，使玉與玉相觸有聲，以節行止，這就是玉藻所說的：「古之君子必佩玉」的玉佩。此外佩玉兼有實用者，則是腰帶上之帶鈎，射器時手指上所戴的玉韘。

鑲嵌玉是鑲在器物上的玉，例如玉璏、玉璲、玉琫、玉珌，是鑲在劍身或劍鞘上的飾物。其他如鑲在杖上的玉杖首，或嵌在帶上的玉帶板，都是經常所見到的。

喪葬玉是一種殉葬的玉，相傳人死之後，把玉放在九竅裏（眼二、鼻二、耳二、口、前後排洩道共九處），屍體就不會腐朽，所以有用玉殉葬之風氣。放在口中的玉，叫做「唅」，放在耳中的玉叫「瑱」，放在手中的玉叫「握」。古塚中出土的「唅」，有很多

是蟬形的，這是因爲蟬的形狀與舌形相似，放在口內較爲合適，這一種玉蟬，也叫作「唅蟬」。

舞樂器用之於歌舞，歌舞是人之天性，古代人遇有可喜的事，自然發出狂歡的歌聲，揮舞着使用的兵器，或擊打器皿發出音響的配合，這樣的演變，玉兵如斧戚之屬，變成了舞樂器。農具中犂的形制，便採用做玉磬的規格了。

其他如文具中的筆架、臂擱、硯池；陳設用的山子、花挿、花薰；仿製的瓜果、蔬菜、人馬、車船，以及盤盌、酒盃、茶壺等，不盡一一列舉。

個別解説

1　商　舊玉鳥紋珮

縱11.35公分　橫5.0公分　厚0.3公分

器身作鳥形。玉呈淡櫻。鏤空琱琢一鳥，作仰首直立狀，短翼長尾，一龍伏於鳥首之上。

2　商　舊玉素璧

徑37.0公分　厚1.36公分

器身作板狀圓形，中心有圓孔。兩面均光素，無紋飾。石紋明顯，似經剖開之後，稍加琢磨而成。玉呈青色，並有櫻色斑，古雅可愛。

3　商　舊玉圭

長30.6公分　最寬7.2公分　厚1.25公分

器身狹長，下有一孔，玉質細潤，色呈櫻赭。一面琱蟬紋，下有鳥紋一道；並鐫篆文「五福五代」一圓璽，及楷書乾隆丙午御題，下有篆文「比德」、「朗潤」方璽二。一面琱鷹紋，兩翼舒張，昂首直立，有一飛冲霄之勢，下方有鳥紋一道；鐫有篆文「古希天子」圓璽一，並有楷書乾隆丙午御題，下有篆文「比德」、「朗潤」方璽二。按圭之形制，以寬而薄者爲上方，清高宗爲便於琢鐫御題詩文，因就其形倒刻。

4　周　舊玉圭

長24.6公分　最寬6.9公分　厚1.22公分

器身狹長，下方有圓孔二，大小各一。玉質細潤，色青含灰，沁染處，一端呈淺櫻，一端呈黑色。一面琱人面紋，上下各鐫有篆方璽二，一爲「五福五代堂古希天子寶」，一爲「太上皇帝之寶」，中有隸書清高宗御題。一面琱獸面紋，鐫有楷書及隸書乾隆御題，各一段。最下有篆文「八徵耄念」方璽一。

5　周　舊玉穀紋璧

厚0.7公分　徑26.4公分

器身作板狀圓形，中心有圓孔。玉呈櫻赭。內圈穀紋，外圍龍紋，兩面花紋均同。

周禮璧爲朝覲六瑞之一，用同於圭，爲子爵所執，形制應爲直徑五寸。然璧之爲用至繁，亦有用薶沉，饋送者，此器由尺寸觀之，當非子爵所執者。

6　周　舊玉琮

高47.2公分　縱橫6.73公分

器身長，作方柱形，口圓中空如筒狀，兩端相通。通體飾有駒紋。玉質細潤，呈櫻褐色。

7　周　舊玉琮

高15.7公分　縱橫7.0公分

器身作方柱形，口圓中空如筒狀，兩端相通。玉呈櫻褐色。通體飾有駒紋。

琮爲禮器，用以祭地者，我國素有「天圓地方」之語，是以用圓璧禮天，方琮禮地。

8　周　舊玉璜

縱6.0公分　橫17.75公分　厚0.55公分

器身作板狀半圓形，色呈櫻赭。兩面均飾穀紋。周側鐫有篆書乾隆乙丑御題。下有篆文「古香」「太樸」方璽二。木座圓心，双面均有銀嵌乾卦及乾隆己丑、庚寅御題。

璜之形爲半璧，其用爲佩飾的，大都琢有花紋；禮器之璜，用作禮北方之神，則用玄色玉製做。

9　周　舊玉斧

長12.7公分　寬5.0公分　厚2.45公分

器身下寬，兩端較薄，側面有一橫穿。兩面均琱琢人面紋。玉質細潤，通體呈櫻色，深淺不同，花紋精細。

斧、本爲兵器，以玉製造者，多爲舞樂器。

10　周　舊玉戚

長23.1公分　最寬14.0公分　厚0.95公分

器板狀體，斧形。玉質瑩澈，色呈櫻褐。琢双龍紋，兩面均同。

戚是兵器的一種，用玉製作，爲舞樂器之用。

11　周　舊玉穀紋環

徑11.1公分　厚0.5公分

器身作板狀圓形，中心圓孔較大，孔徑與爾雅所說「肉好若一」之比例相合。玉質晶瑩，沁處呈櫻褐色。兩面均飾穀紋。

環之用，多作爲佩飾；有關於符節者，則如廣韻所說：「逐臣待命於境，賜環則返，賜玦則絕。」是取「環」音與「還」同。

12　周　舊玉環

　　　　　　　　　　　　　　　　　　　　　　　　徑17.15公分　　厚0.4公分

器身作板狀圓形，兩面均琱蒲紋。玉質瑩澈，色黃泛青，沁處呈淺櫻色。

13　戰國　舊玉系璧　五件

　　系璧、是佩飾用之小璧，說文註：「系璧、蓋爲小璧，系帶間左右佩物也。」
系璧之尺寸與紋飾，均無限制，而隨各人之愛好，惟大致均不離璧形。

　　　　　　　　　　　　　　　　　　　　　　　　徑6.67公分　　厚0.6公分

一、器身作板狀圓形，中心有孔，兩面光素。玉色青，沁處呈櫻色。

　　　　　　　　　　　　　　　　　　　　縱6.25公分　　橫4.9公分　　厚0.7公分

二、器身作橢圓環狀，兩面光素，玉質細潤色青，沁呈淺櫻色。

　　　　　　　　　　　　　　　　　　　　　　　　徑5.27公分　　厚0.6公分

三、器身作板狀圓形，中心有孔，兩面琱琢雲紋。玉色青，沁處呈深櫻色。

　　　　　　　　　　　　　　　　　　　　　　　　徑4.42公分　　厚0.4公分

四、器身作板狀圓形，中心圓孔，兩面光素。玉質細潤色青，沁處呈淺櫻
　　色。

　　　　　　　　　　　　　　　　　　　　縱4.2公分　　橫3.76公分　　厚0.46公分

五、器身作長圓形，邊緣較薄，中心有孔，兩面光素。玉色青綠，沁處呈櫻
　　色。

14　戰國　舊玉珩

　　　　　　　　　　　　　　　　　　　　縱2.8公分　　橫20.2公分　　厚0.55公分

器身作扁平半圓形，上方有一孔，兩端均有凹槽。兩面琢雲紋。玉質晶澈，
沁處呈櫻赭色。

　　珩屬於服御器，爲玉珮之主幹部份，下垂不同之雜珮，說文云：「珩、佩上
玉也、所以節行止也。」

15　漢　舊玉蠶紋璧

　　　　　　　　　　　　　　　　　　　　　　　　徑19.8公分　　厚0.8公分

　　器身作板狀圓形，中心圓孔。兩面均琢琱蠶紋。玉色青白細潤，受沁處呈櫻
褐色。周緣鐫篆書乾隆乙未御題，下有篆文「乾」、「隆」連珠方璽。

16　漢　舊玉蟬紋瑗

　　　　　　　　　　　　　　　　　　　　　　　　徑15.02公分　　厚0.75公分

器身板狀圓形，孔徑頗大。一面琱蟬紋，一面琱龍紋。玉質細潤，色青泛

綠，沁處呈深樓及樓褐色。周緣鐫篆書乾隆壬子御題，下有篆文「古香」、「太樸」二小璽。

瑗、具有「援引」之意，荀子云：「召人以瑗。」

17　漢　舊玉璏、璲、璲、珌

璏、璲、璲、珌四器，均屬於鑲嵌玉，璏、鑲於劍靶之頂端，璲、鑲於劍身與劍柄之間，璲、嵌於鞘身，珌、鑲於鞘之下方。

徑5.1公分

璏、器身作板狀，平面圓形。面琱穀紋，背部光素，中心有槽，以裝置劍靶。玉色含青，沁處呈樓褐色。

縱2.22公分　橫6.53公分

璲、器身上下兩端似稜形，上端中間凹進，下方中有尖峰，器心有扁形穿孔。一面琱獸面紋，一面琱螭紋，螭首為浮琱。

縱10.27公分　橫2.7公分

璲、器身如帶，兩端微捲。面上浮琱雙螭紋，背部光素，有方銎。玉質溫潤，沁處呈樓褐色。

縱4.88公分　橫5.72公分

珌、器身上窄下濶，兩端面平狀如梭形，上端中心有一淺圓孔。兩面均琱雲紋。玉質細潤，沁處呈淺樓色。

18　漢　舊玉帶頭

縱6.1公分　橫9.55公分　厚2.16公分

器身略呈長方，上端較寬作圓形，邊緣有象鼻孔，以便與帶連綴。面上浮琱龜紋及螭紋，背部光素。玉質瑩細，色白含青，沁處呈樓色。

帶頭，屬於鑲嵌器，飾於帶之一端。

19　漢　舊玉唅蟬　八件

唅蟬為喪葬之器，為放入死人口中之玉，相傳人死之後，將玉放置九竅，則尸體不朽，所以有用玉殉葬之風。器身均作蟬形，上濶下銳，光素未加紋飾。

長6.11公分　寬2.97公分　厚0.82公分

一、玉色青，沁處呈白褐。

長6.02公分　寬2.92公分　厚0.9公分

二、玉色白中含青，沁處呈淺樓色。

長6.0公分　寬3.2公分　厚1.23公分

三、玉色沁呈淺櫻。

長4.67公分　寬2.75公分　厚1.0公分

四、玉質瑩白，沁處呈櫻色。

長6.67公分　寬3.45公分　厚0.67公分

五、玉沁處呈淺櫻及櫻褐色。

長5.03公分　寬2.55公分　厚0.68公分

六、玉色青，沁處呈櫻褐色。

長5.85公分　寬2.92公分　厚0.5公分

七、玉色青，沁處微呈淺櫻色。

長5.87公分　寬3.19公分　厚0.87公分

八、玉色白中泛青，沁處呈深櫻色。

20　漢　舊玉辟邪

最高9.6公分　最長13.2公分　最寬3.55公分

器身作獸形，有兩角雙翼，昂首張口，長尾曳地，口足直立作欲行之狀，神態凶猛。玉質經土華浸染，色呈櫻赭，古樸斑爛，精美雅緻。胸前鐫有隸書銀嵌乾隆甲午御題，下有篆文「太樸」方璽一。

辟邪爲古代傳說中的異獸，大都置於墓前，古人以「辟邪」之名，有「辟除邪惡」之意，因以用玉製器，饋贈友人。

21　漢　墨玉牧羝器架

高11.5公分　長15.7公分　寬6.9公分

器身爲羊形，作跪伏之狀。羊背後端飾一牧人，與羊首對稱，器身中段凹入，似爲他物之架座。玉黑潤，色極美。底鐫隸書乾隆丁亥御題，下有篆文「比德」、「朗潤」方璽二。

22　宋　舊玉單把栝

高12.2公分　口徑4.7公分　足徑3.14公分　通鋬徑6.6公分

器直口，深壁，短足，腹壁有環形鋬。通體滿作雲紋，口部琢獸面紋。沁染處，口呈綠色，足作淺褐。

23　宋　舊玉蟠龍觥

高14.6公分　縱5.8公分　橫11.79公分

器身作龍首狀，首向下，有龍首鋬。口內邊緣鐫有篆書乾隆壬寅御題，下有篆文「比德」、「朗潤」小璽二。玉色瑩白含青，沁處呈櫻色。

61

觥爲酒器，古以角爲之，後改用銅，此器則用玉仿製。

24　明　白玉秋蟬桐葉洗

高6.0公分　縱14.3公分　橫20.7公分

器身作一片桐葉，滿飾筋絡，邊緣處琢有蟲嚙之痕，極爲肖眞；葉旁襯以折枝，枝上有葉數片，一秋蟬棲於枝上，玉質瑩澈，色白含青。

洗爲文具之一，爲畫家所必需，此器鏤空透琱，形制精美。

25　明　白玉鰲魚花挿

高15.6公分　縱4.26公分　橫9.55公分

器身作一魚形，口微侈，深腹。玉質晶瑩，呈青白色，邊緣之處，則呈黑色。魚雙睛努出，首生雙角，鬚、頰、翅、鰭俱備，通體飾鱗紋，尾部曲折，下方襯以波濤；魚身似自水中躍出之狀，口部張開，卽利用魚口爲瓶口，腹部飾一小龍。

花挿爲陳設品，可用以挿花。此器之製法，利用玉身之色澤，施以巧琢，通稱爲「巧作」。

26　清　白玉茶壺

通蓋高10.7公分　縱10.25公分　橫16.8公分

器身作圓形壺，歛口，深壁，矮圈足，有鋬、鋬。通體光素無紋飾，鋬爲鳳首，鋬作如意形；蓋面光素，蓋頂作蓮花。底鐫隸書「嘉慶御用」四字款。玉質潤澤瑩潔，色白含青。

27　清　白玉四耳彝爐

通蓋高12.8公分　縱15.4公分　橫17.1公分

器身作圓形，侈口，矮壁，腹微碩，底圈淺凹，下飾四足。琱有四龍形耳，各有一活環；蓋頂端鐫篆書一壽字，圍以四如意耳，玉質瑩潤，色白含青，爲禮佛之器。

28　清　白玉花薰

通蓋高12.9公分　口徑13.4公分　通耳徑19.3公分

器身圓形，侈口，深壁，矮圈足。浮琱鏤空牡丹雙耳，蓋、器通體均滿鏤空透琱牡丹。玉質瑩白含青，形製精美，用盛鮮花，使滿室生香。

29　清　白玉瑞獸尊

高22.1公分　縱4.56公分　橫15.22公分

器身作麒麟，背負扁方瓶，侈口，深壁，腹微碩。有象首雙耳，各銜一活環，頸飾蕉葉紋，腹作雲紋。獸頂有獨角。玉色潔白。

口沿鐫有隸書「大清乾隆仿古」六字款。

30　清　白玉螭耳桮

通耳高5.2公分　縱7.4公分　橫12.56公分

器身作橢圓形，侈口，矮壁，淺圈足。浮琱一螭形耳，口銜靈芝；口沿亦浮琱蟠螭，下襯流雲，器壁光素。玉質晶瑩，螭身利用玉皮爲之。

31　清　青玉蓮藕洗

高8.63公分　縱3.2公分　橫30.9公分

器身作荷、蓮、蓬心諸形，以藕相連，成爲一體，而以一大荷葉爲洗。玉色瑩潔，白中泛青，形制甚美。

32　清　白玉錦荔枝

高8.45公分　縱4.83公分　橫12.31公分

錦荔枝俗稱苦瓜。此器琱錦荔枝二，相連一體，綴以藤葉及小錦荔枝一。玉色潔白，形制逼眞。

33　清　青玉爐

通蓋高12.3公分　縱13.5公分　通耳橫18.0公分

器身作圓形，侈口，矮壁，底呈圓狀，下有三短足。有獸形雙耳，腹壁琱獸面紋，三足上端亦琱獸首；蓋頂作鏤空蟠龍。玉色青。

34　清　碧玉雙耳活環菊瓣洗

通耳高8.3公分　口徑25.4公分　通耳徑35.1公分

器身作圓形，侈口，矮壁，平底，有四短足。通體作菊花紋，琱菊瓣四層，以花蕊爲中心；有蝴蝶雙耳，耳下各有一活環。

底心鐫隸書「乾隆年製」四字款。

35　清　青玉天雞蓋尊

通蓋高19.2公分　縱3.72公分　橫9.12公分

器身琱鳳鳥一隻，背負一瓶，直口，深壁，腹微碩。鳳棲於雙輪之上，長尾內捲。係仿古銅天雞尊之形。

口沿鎸篆書「乾隆年製」四字款。

36　清　碧玉琱秋山獵騎圖筆筒

高18.1公分　徑18.2公分

器身作圓柱形，口壁垂直，深壁，底淺凹，周壁浮琱秋山獵騎圖。口沿下鎸楷書「秋山獵騎」四字。口沿鎸楷書乾隆壬寅御題，下有篆文「會心不遠」方璽一。玉色澤俱佳，紋飾琱琢精細。

筆筒為文具器，用以盛文房四寶之一之筆者，列置几案陳設，亦可供作雅玩。

37　清　碧玉琱龍三足鼎

通蓋高14.4公分　口徑11.25公分　通耳徑17.7公分

器身作圓形，侈口，矮壁，底呈圓狀，下有三短足。有龍形雙耳，腹壁琱獸面紋，飾回紋地；三足上方作獅首，下方為獸爪。蓋面亦琱獸面紋，頂鏤琱蟠龍。器裏光素。玉色澤光潤，花紋精緻。

38　清　碧玉鰲魚花揷

高16.7公分　縱3.6公分　橫11.0公分

器身作魚形，侈口，深壁，底淺凹。琱魚二，大小各一，均作跳躍狀。玉質晶瑩，色呈深綠。為插花之具。

口下鎸篆書「乾隆年製」四字款。

39　清　碧玉尊

通蓋高21.6公分　縱4.6公分　橫12.2公分

器身作異獸形，背負一瓶，侈口，深壁，濶肩，削腹，獸昂首張口，神態凶猛。玉色深綠，形制極美。

口沿鎸篆書「乾隆年製」四字款。

40　清　碧玉鏤空雲龍大香筒

高77.5公分　徑12.7公分

器身作圓柱形，中空似筒狀，通體滿琱鏤空雲紋，一龍蟠繞其上，色呈深綠。

41　清　碧玉蟠龍洗

通高7.4公分　縱9.4公分　橫13.38公分

器身作不規則之橢圓形，歛口，深壁。通體滿琱雲紋，口緣浮琱蟠龍二。
珠上鐫有楷書「乾隆年製」四字款。

42　清　碧玉琱花龍耳爐

通蓋高13.2公分　縱7.4公分　橫16.5公分

器身作長方形，口壁垂直，深壁，平底，下有四短足。蓋面四角各琱一蟠
龍，頂鏤琱蟠龍；腹壁滿琱獸面紋；有龍形雙耳，底光素。琱琢精細。

43　清　黃玉連環鈕印

器身作印三方，一方作橢圓形，二方爲方形，印上端各有鼻鈕‧鈕上各有小
鍊一條，鍊端以小環使三鍊相連，以合成一體。

一、高3.81公分　縱2.39公分　橫3.41公分
二、高3.46公分　縱2.65公分　橫2.68公分
三、高3.42公分　縱2.65公分　橫2.66公分

鍊長16.8公分

44　清　翠玉松鶴山子

高14.0公分　縱4.2公分　橫11.33公分

用翠玉琱爲山子，正面峯巒聳翠，石磴流泉，喬松鶴鹿，長春之景。背面山
石鱗峋，峯勢縱橫，頗饒清趣。

45　清　翠玉白菜

長18.7公分　縱5.07公分　橫9.1公分

用翠玉琱爲白菜，依玉之原色施以巧琢，以綠色部份琢爲菜葉，白色處施作
菜身，酷似實物，葉上浮琱螽斯蟲二。

46　清　翠玉松鶴插屏

長21.63公分　寬15.4公分　厚1.05公分

器身作板狀長方形，一面琱松鶴遐齡；一面琱壽山福海。玉呈翠綠。

47　清　紅瑪瑙蟠桃洗

高9.9公分　縱6.15公分　最寬8.83公分

器身琱爲樹幹一段，深壁，平底。幹旁浮琱枝葉，蟠折轉繞於器側，枝上結

有一桃實，口緣處有一蝙蝠，口銜靈芝。器身通體呈紅色，惟蝙蝠爲白色，紅白相映，美麗異常。

48　清　瑪瑙磨具

通高15.4公分　縱20.9公分　通鑾鑿徑25.9公分

用瑪瑙琱琢磨具一套，色灰，間有紅、黑斑點、磨圓式，形制肖眞。

49　清　墨晶筆筒

高16.6公分　縱8.7公分　橫11.61公分

器身琱爲古松老幹，深壁，平底。兩側浮琱枝朷，幹身散佈松鱗。口沿下鐫有草書題識。文曰：「松至千年能化石，此身原不愧徂來。」晶呈墨色，形制精美。

50　清　肉形石

高5.73公分　縱5.3公分　橫6.6公分

器爲天然豬肉形石，酷似臘肉，面上毛孔星佈，皮下肥瘦相間，狀甚逼眞。

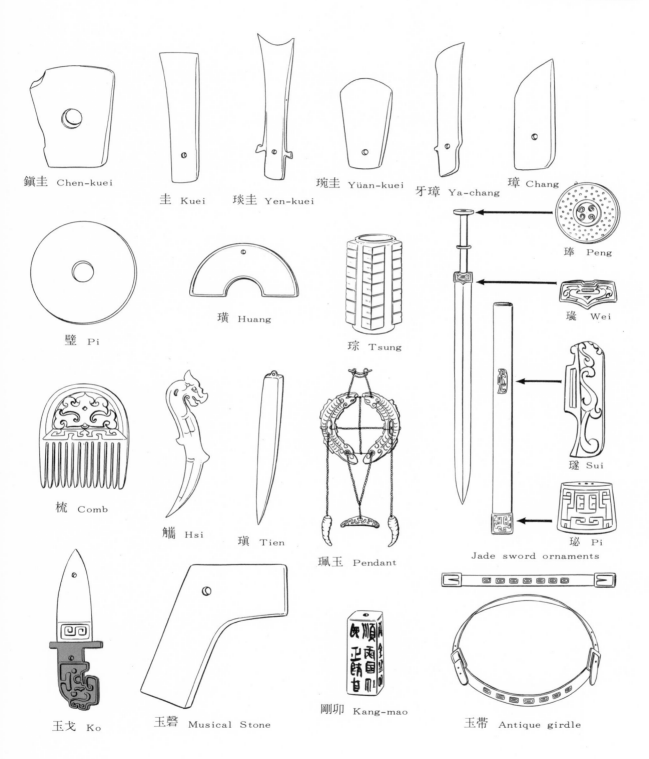

鎮圭 Chen-kuei

圭 Kuei

琰圭 Yen-kuei

琬圭 Yüan-kuei

牙璋 Ya-chang

璋 Chang

琫 Peng

璏 Wei

璧 Pi

璜 Huang

琮 Tsung

璲 Sui

梳 Comb

觽 Hsi

瑱 Tien

珌 Pi

珮玉 Pendant

Jade sword ornaments

玉戈 Ko

玉磬 Musical Stone

剛卯 Kang-mao

玉带 Antique girdle

玉　器

　玉は石の一種であり、半透明で、肌は温潤で光沢があるため、『説文解字』という中国の古典では、玉を「石の美なるもの」と説明している。しかし、美しい石は玉ばかりではない。ルビー、サファイア、トルコ石、青金石、金緑石、瑪瑙、水晶など、みな同様に美しい光沢をもっている。もっとも、これらはいずれも古人が玉を広義に表現したもので、美しい石はすべて玉といったものと思われる。鉱物学的には、白玉、青玉、黄玉、碧玉、墨玉などの軟玉と、硬玉、つまりダイヤ、ルビー、翡翠などの二種類に大別される。

　いわゆる広義の玉の産出地については、古典に数多く記載されているが、鉱物学にいう玉は、中国では新疆省から軟玉が、雲南省からは硬玉が産出している。

　玉は非常に硬いので、彫刻、研磨して器にするのは容易ではない。中国では数千年来、ごく簡単な道具を使って、多種多様の精密、美麗な器を作ってきたが、これは世界に誇る中国の伝統的な「琢玉工芸」の所産にほかならない。

　玉器は、石器の製法から生まれた。人類はやがて銅を発見し、銅器を使うようになり、石器の実用性はうすれた。それでも人々は長年人類の幸福に寄与した石器を捨て去るにしのびず、石器を記念して、これを祭祀の対象として尊び、玉で石器を模造して、人類永遠のしるしとした。そして聡明な統治者たちは、こういう人々の心理をつかんで、石斧、石鎌の形にのっとって朝廷の礼器を制定した。

　玉で作られた器物は三種類に大別される。

　一つは祭祀品として礼拝の対象とされるもの、一つは朝廷で使用される礼器、他の一つは民衆の装飾器、喪葬器などである。人類は古来、新奇と進歩を追求してきた。器物が実用のためでなく、一種の芸術的作品として作られた場合、必然的に長い時間とおびただしい人力を使って最高最美の作品が作られるようになる。こうして玉器の製作技術もしだいに進歩し、美的領域にまで到達した。伝来の古代器物にみられる彫刻、研磨の精巧さは、現代の私たちを驚嘆させる。それらの製作技術は、数千年を経てなおみずみずしく精彩がある。

　礼器は玉で作られたが、重要なものは「六端」と「六器」である。「六瑞」とは、政府により規定された各種寸法の圭と璧をさ

し、国内の最高の爵位をもつ人に授与され、彼らの権力を象徴する。鎮圭（ちん）、桓圭（かん）、信圭（しん）、躬圭（きゅう）はそれぞれ天子、公爵、侯爵、伯爵が所有し、その形制は同じだが、寸法の長短により尊卑の順序が分別される。穀璧（こく）、蒲璧（は）はそれぞれ子爵と男爵が所有し、やはり形制は変わらないが、文飾により分別される。

「六器」とは、天子が天地四方を礼祭するために使用する祭祀器をさす。蒼璧、黄琮（そう）は天と地を祭るときに使用し、青圭、赤璋（しょう）、白琥（こ）、玄璜（こう）は東、南、西、北の四方を祭るときに使用された。これらの名称の第一字は玉の色彩を、第二字は器の種類をあらわしている。たとえば、蒼璧とは蒼色の玉で作った璧で、蒼は天の色、「蒼々たるものは天」のそれである。黄琮は黄色の玉で作られ、中国の大地すなわち黄土の意味である。中国に「天円地方」ということばがある。天は円く地は四角という意味で、円い璧で天を祭り、四角な琮で地を祭った。そのほか四方を祭る玉の形は「五行の説」により図案化されている。

「符節器」とは、玉が命令を下すときに使用する信符（手形）であり、凶、荒、危、乱の際、天子は官吏に符節をもたせて現地に派遣し王命を伝達した。珍圭（ちん）、琰圭（えん）、琬圭（わん）、穀圭（こく）などはみなこの符節器に属し、「不法を征伐する」「善行を表彰する」「紛争を調停する」など、おのおのその規定による使命をもっている。牙璋（がしょう）は派兵専用の符節である。もっとも、これらの符節は単純な形のと玉器で、たやすく偽造できたので、純朴な上古の時代はともかく、東周以後は「虎符」に改正し、虎形の符節を二つに割って政府と将軍が片方ずつ保持し、調達のときは命令を受け取った者が二片を一つに合わせて真偽を確かめる方法がとられた。

佩飾玉（はいしょく）とは、佩帯用の飾り物で、頭や首、腰などに帯びる装飾品である。身につける飾り物は、はじめは獣の牙や鳥の骨の類が使われたが、のち玉をそれらの形に細工して用いた。玉觿（けい）、円瑹（きん）はその形が獣牙と骨管によく似ている。玉笄（けい）、玉珩（こう）、系璧（けいへき）、鳥獣文佩（はい）などもみな佩玉である。翁仲（おうちゅう）と剛卯（ごうぼう）はともに佩玉であると同時に一種の呪い品（まじな）でもあった。当時は数個の玉を連ねたものを腰に帯びていた。歩くと玉と玉がふれあって音をたてる。それにより行動に節度をもたせ、ものごしをみやびにした。これは『礼記』の「玉藻」という篇に、「昔の君子は必ず玉を佩びる」と書かれている玉佩のことである。ほかに佩玉と実用を兼ねた腰帯の

帯鈎、弓を射るとき手指にはめる玉鞢などもある。

　鑲嵌玉というのは器物の上に象嵌された玉をいう。玉琫、玉璏、玉璲、玉珌などは、刀身や剣鞘の上に象嵌された飾り物である。そのほか杖に象嵌された玉杖首、帯にはめられた玉帯板はよく見られるものである。

　喪葬玉は一種の殉葬の玉である。伝えによれば、人の死後、玉を九竅（眼2、鼻2、耳2、口、前と後ろの排泄道の計9か所）におけば、死体は腐朽しないといい、玉を殉葬用にした習慣があった。口の中においた玉を「琀」、耳の中においた玉を「瑱」、手中においた玉を「握」という。古墳の中から出土した「琀」は蟬形が多い。これは蟬の形が舌の形に似ていて、口の中に入れてしっくりするからで、この種の玉蟬は「琀蟬」ともいわれる。

　舞楽器は歌舞の際に使う。歌踊は人の天性で、古代の人は喜ばしいときは自然に狂歓の歌声を発し、手にもった兵器で舞い踊り、あるいは皿や小鉢をたたいて和した。こうして斧戚のような玉兵に属するものでも舞楽器に使われてしまう。農具の「犁」の形は、玉磬の規格を採用したものである。

　そのほか玉で、文房具類の筆立、腕枕、硯、陳列用の山岳形、花瓶、香炉、瓜果や蔬菜形、人馬、車船、さらに盤盌、酒盃、茶壺を作るなど、逐一列挙するにいとまがない。

作品解説

1　商　旧玉鳥文珮 _{はい}

縦 11.35cm　横 5.0cm　厚さ 0.3cm

器は鳥形で、玉は薄茶色を呈する。透彫りで、首をあげ直立した鳥が一羽彫ってある。その翼は短く、尾は長い。鳥の首の上には一匹の龍が載っている。

2　商　旧玉素璧 _{そへき}

径 37.0cm　厚さ 1.36cm

器は板状の円形で、中心にまるい孔がある。両面ともに素面で光沢があり、文様はない。地文がはっきりみえるのは、切断されてから多少琢磨したためであろう。玉は青色を呈し、茶色の斑点がある。古雅愛すべきである。

3　商　旧玉圭 _{けい}

長さ 30.6cm　最広幅 7.2cm　厚さ 1.25cm

器身は細長く、上に一つ孔がある。玉質は細かくつやがあり、茶褐色を呈する。一面には蟬文が彫られ、上に鳥文一筋と、篆文で「五福五代」の四字の円璽一つ、さらに楷書の乾隆丙午（1786）の御題詩とその下に篆文で「比徳」「朗潤」の方璽二つが彫ってある。また他の一面には、両翼をひろげ、首を直立し、ひと飛び雲の上までといった趣の鷹文、その下に鳥文が一筋あり、篆文で「古希天子」の円璽、それに楷書の乾隆丙午御題詩の下に篆文で「比徳」「朗潤」の二つの方璽がそれぞれ彫られている。

ちなみに、圭の形式では、広くて薄いほうが上ということになっているが、清の高宗皇帝は、御題の詩文を彫るのに便利なように、圭をさかさまにして彫刻している。

4　周　旧玉圭 _{けい}

長さ 24.6cm　最広幅 6.9cm　厚さ 1.22cm

器は細長く、上方に大小二つのまるい孔がある。玉質は細かくつややかで、やや灰色がかった青色を呈し、しみのある部分は一端が薄茶で他の一端は黒い。一面には人面文を彫り、上下にそれぞれ篆文で「五福五代堂古希天子寶」「太上皇帝之寶」の方璽二つが彫られ、中に隷書で清の乾隆帝の御題がある。他の一面は獣面文で、乾隆帝の御題が楷書と隷書で一段ずつ彫られている。一番下には篆文で「八徵耄念」の方璽が一つある。

5　周　旧玉穀文璧 _{へき}

径 26.4cm　厚さ 0.7cm

器は板状の円形で、中心にまるい孔がある。玉の色は茶褐色で、両面とも内側に穀文があり、外側を龍文でかこんでいる。

周礼に璧は朝観六瑞の一つで、圭と同じように用いられ、子爵の所持するも

のとされて、形状としては直径五寸と定められている。しかし璧の用途は多く、中には祭礼用として山河に埋沈したり、または贈答に使うこともあった。この器は、その寸法の大きさにより、必ずしも子爵の所持するものではないと判断される。

6　周　旧玉琮(そう)

高さ 47.2cm　縦横共 6.73cm

器は長い方柱形で、上はまるく、中は空で、筒抜けの筒状になっている。器全体は駔文(そう)（組紐をかける突起、わが国では俗に八卦文という）で飾られ、玉質は細かくつややかで、茶褐色を呈する。

琮は礼器で、地を祭るときに使う。中国では「天は円く地は四角」ということばがあるように、まるい璧をもって天を祭り、四角の琮をもって地を祭った。

7　周　旧玉琮(そう)

高さ 15.7cm　縦横共 7.0cm

器は方柱形で、口はまるく、中は空で、筒状をなし、いわゆる筒抜けになっている。玉は茶褐色で、器全体に駔文がある。

8　周　旧玉璜(こう)

縦 6.0cm　横 17.75cm　厚さ 0.55cm

器は板状の半円形で、色は茶褐色である。両面ともに穀文がある。周側に篆書で乾隆乙丑の御題が彫ってある。その下に篆文で「古香」「太樸」の方璽二つがある。木製硯屏の中心座は円心で、両面ともに銀で乾卦が嵌(は)められ、乾隆乙丑、庚寅の御題がある。

璜の形は半璧になっており、佩飾に使われ、多くの花文が彫られている。礼器の璜は、北方の神を祭るときには必ず暗黒色の玉で作られた。

9　周　旧玉斧(ふ)

長さ 12.7cm　幅 5.0cm　厚さ 2.45cm

器は下のほうが広く、両端はやや薄く、側面に一本の横穿（横つなぎ）がある。両面には人面文が彫られ、玉質は細潤である。器全体は茶色で、濃い部分と薄い部分があり、花文は大変精巧である。

斧(おの)そのものは兵器であり、玉で作られているものの、多くは舞楽器として用いた。

10　周　旧玉戚(せき)

長さ 23.1cm　最広幅 14.0cm　厚さ 0.95cm

器は板状で斧の形をし、玉質は半透明で潤いがあり、茶褐色を呈する。両面

とも双龍文が彫られている。戚は兵器の一種であるが、これは玉で作られ、舞楽器として使われた。

11 周 旧玉穀文環

径 11.1cm 厚さ 0.5cm

器は板状円形で、中心のまるい孔は比較的大きい。孔径は『爾雅』でいう「肉好若一」のように、比例は一致している（「肉と好は一のごとし」とは「地の径幅と孔の径幅は同じ寸法」の意味）。玉質は半透明で明るく、しみの部分は茶褐色をしている。両面ともに穀文がある。

環はおもに佩飾として用いられた。符節（割符）として使ったのは、『廣韻』に「放逐された臣は国境で君命を待っており、環を与えられたら帰り、玦を与えられたら帰らない」とあるように、「環」の音をとって「還」（帰る）と同じ意味に使ったものである。

12 周 旧玉環

径 17.15cm 厚さ 0.4cm

器は板状の円形で、両面ともに薄文がある。玉質は半透明で潤いがあり、色は黄であるが青みをおびている。しみの部分は淡い茶色を呈している。

13 戦国 旧玉系璧 五件

系璧とは、佩飾用の小璧をさす。『説文解字』の注にも、「系璧とは皆小璧をいい、腰の帯の近くに佩用するものなり」とある。系璧の寸法と文飾には別に定めはなく、各人の好みによったが、おおむね璧の形を離れていない。

上右 器は板状の円形で、中心に孔がある。両面とも素面で光沢がある。玉は青色で、しみの部分は茶色を呈している。 　径 6.01cm 厚さ 0.6cm

下左 器は楕円の環状で、両面とも線文で光沢があり、玉質は細かくつややかで色は青い。しみの部分は淡い茶色を呈している。

縦 6.25cm 横 4.9cm 厚さ 0.7cm

上左 器は板状の円形で、中心に孔があり、両面ともに雲紋が彫られている。玉は青色で、しみの部分は深い茶色を呈している。

径 5.27cm 厚さ 0.6cm

下中 器は板状の円形で、中心にまるい孔があり、両面は素面で光沢がある。玉質は細かくつややかで、しみの部分は淡い茶色を呈している。

径 4.42cm 厚さ 0.4cm

下右 器は長円形で、縁は比較的薄く、中心に孔があり、両面は素面で光沢がある。玉は青緑色で、しみの部分は茶色を呈している。

縦 4.2cm 横 3.76cm 厚さ 0.46cm

14　戦国　旧玉珩

縦 2.8cm　横 20.2cm　厚さ 0.55cm

器は平たい半円形で、上に孔一つがあり、両端ともにくぼんだ槽（くりこみ）がある。両面には雲文が彫られ、玉質は半透明で明るく、しみの部分は茶褐色を呈する。

珩とは服御の器であり、玉珮の主要部分をなし、下にいろいろの雑珮が垂れている。『説文解字』には、「珩とは佩上の玉なり、もって行止を節する」と説明されている。

15　漢　旧玉蚕文璧

径 19.8cm　厚さ 0.8cm

器は板状の円形で、中心にまるい孔があり、両面ともに蚕文が彫ってある。玉は青白色で、玉質は細かくつやがあり、しみの部分は茶色を呈する。周縁に篆書で乾隆乙未（1775）の御題が彫られ、下に篆文で「乾」「隆」の連珠の方璽がある。

16　漢　旧玉蟬文瑗

径 15.02cm　厚さ 0.75cm

板状の円形で、孔の径が非常に大きい。一面には蟬文が彫られ、他の一面には龍文がある。玉質は細かくつややかで、緑がかった青色を呈し、しみの部分は濃い茶と茶褐色を示す。周縁に篆書の乾隆壬子（1792）の御題が、下に篆文で「古香」「太樸」の二つの小璽がある。

瑗には「援引（応用する）」の意味があり、荀子は「召人以瑗」といっている。

17　漢　旧玉琫、璏、璲、珌

琫、璏、璲、珌の四種はともに象嵌玉であり、琫は剣の柄の上端に、璏は剣身と剣柄の中間に、璲は鞘の身に、珌は鞘の下方にはめ込まれる玉である。

上右　琫　器は板状、平面円形をなし、表には穀文がある。裏は無文で光沢がある中心に槽（くりこみ）があって、剣の柄にとりつけるようになっている。色は青みがかっており、しみの部分は茶褐色である。

径 5.1cm

下右　璏　上下両端は棱（かど）形で、上端の中間はくぼんでおり、下方の中心に尖峰があり、器の中を扁形の孔が通っている。一面に獣面文、他の面に螭文が彫られ、螭首は浮彫りになっている。

縦 2.22cm　横 6.53cm

上左　璲　両端が帯のようにやや巻いている。面には浮彫りの双螭文があり、背面は素面で光沢のある無文で、四角の釜がある。玉質はつやや

かで、しみの部分は茶褐色をしている。　　　　縦 10.27cm　横 2.7cm

下左　玼　上方は狭く下方は広い。両端面は平らかで、梭（おさ）のようにとがって
　　　いる。上端の中央に一つ浅いまるい孔がある。両面に雲文がある。玉
　　　質は細かくつややかで、しみの部分は淡い茶色を呈している。

　　　　　　　　　　　　　　　　　　　　　　縦 4.88cm　横（底）5.72cm

18　漢　旧玉帯頭

　　　　　　　　　　　　　　　縦 6.1cm　横 9.55cm　厚さ 2.16cm

　やや長方形で、一端は広くまるい。縁には象鼻（しょうび）の孔があり、帯に連ねるよう
になっている。表面には浮彫りの亀文と螭文があり、背部は無文で光沢がある。
玉質はこまやかで、青みがかった白色で、しみの部分は茶色を呈している。
　帯頭は象嵌器に属し、帯の一端に飾りつけ、留める用をなす。

19　漢　旧玉唅蟬（がんせん）　八件

　唅蟬は喪葬の器である。死人の口中に入れる玉で、伝えによると、人の死
後、玉を九竅（きょう）（九つの穴）に入れておくと死体が窩朽しないというので、玉を
殉葬する習慣が生まれたといわれる。器はみな蟬形で、上は広く下はとがって
おり無文で光沢がある。
下中右　青色で、しみの部分は白褐色を呈する。

　　　　　　　　　　　　　　　長さ 6.11cm　幅 2.97cm　厚さ 0.82cm
上中右　青みがかった白色で、しみの部分は淡い茶色を呈する。

　　　　　　　　　　　　　　　長さ 6.02cm　幅 2.92cm　厚さ 0.9cm
上中左　しみの部分が淡い茶色を呈している。

　　　　　　　　　　　　　　　長さ 6.0cm　幅 3.2cm　厚さ 1.23cm
上右　白色で、しみの部分は茶色。　　　長さ 4.67cm　幅 2.75cm　厚さ 1.0cm
下中左　しみの部分は淡い茶色および茶褐色。

　　　　　　　　　　　　　　　長さ 6.67cm　幅 3.45cm　厚さ 0.67cm
下左　青色で、しみの部分は茶褐色を呈する。

　　　　　　　　　　　　　　　長さ 5.03cm　幅 2.55cm　厚さ 0.68cm
上左　青色で、しみの部分はやや淡い茶色を呈する。

　　　　　　　　　　　　　　　長さ 5.85cm　幅 2.92cm　厚さ 0.5cm
下右　青みがかった白色で、しみの部分は濃い茶色を呈する。

　　　　　　　　　　　　　　　長さ 5.87cm　幅 3.19cm　厚さ 0.87cm

20　漢　旧玉辟邪（へきじゃ）

　　　　　　　　　　　　　　　高さ 9.6cm　長さ 13.2cm　幅 3.55cm

　獣形で、二つの角と二つの翼がある。首をあげ、口を張り、長い尾は地を引
き、四つ足で直立し、まさに行動に移ろうとする勇猛の姿勢を示している。玉

質は土のしみにより茶褐色となり、古色素朴で、文様、形ともに精美でみやびやかな趣がある。胸部に隷書銀象嵌の乾隆甲午（1774）の御題があり、その下に篆文で「太樸」の方璽一つがある。

辟邪は古代伝説中の奇獣で、主として墓前に供えられる。辟邪には「邪悪を取り除く」意味があり、古人はこれを玉でつくり友人に贈答した。

21　漢　墨玉牧瓶器架

高さ 11.5cm　長さ 15.7cm　幅 6.9cm

羊がひざまずく形をしている。後背部に牧人がひとり羊首と背向かいに坐っている。器身の中央はくぼんでいて、ここに物をもたせかけたらしい。玉は黒くつややかで美しい。底部に隷書で「乾隆丁亥御題」（丁亥は1767）と彫られ、その下に篆文で「比徳」「朗潤」の方璽二つがある。

22　宋　旧玉単把栝

高さ 12.2cm　口径 4.7cm　足径 3.14cm

把手までの幅 6.6cm

直口で、壁は深く足は短い。腹壁に環形の把手がついている。全体は雲文で飾られ、口部に獣面文がある。しみの部分は、口が緑色、足は浅褐色を呈している。

23　宋　旧玉蟠龍觥

高さ 14.6cm　縦 5.8cm　横 11.79cm

器は全体が龍首の形をしており、首は下を向く。また別の龍首の把手がついている。口の内縁に篆書で「乾隆壬寅御題」（壬寅は1782）が彫られ、下に篆文で「比徳」「朗潤」の小璽二つがある。玉は青みがかった明るい白色で、しみの部分は茶色を呈する。

觥は酒器で、古代は獣角で作られたが、のち銅にかわった。この器は玉で模造したものである。

24　明　白玉秋蟬桐葉洗

高さ 6.0cm　縦 14.3cm　横 20.7cm

桐の一葉で、全面に葉脈をほどこし、辺縁には虫の食ったあとまで彫ってあり、本物の葉そっくりである。また葉のわきに小枝をそえ、枝の上に数片の葉があり、枝元には秋蟬が一匹とまっている。玉質は透明で明るい。色は白く、青みがかっている。

洗は文具の一種で、書画家・文人が用いる。この器は鏤空（透彫り）で、形が精巧にできている。

25　明　白玉鰲魚花插

高さ 15.6cm　縦 4.26cm　横 9.55cm

　魚の形をし、口はやや広く、腹が太い。玉質は明るく青白い。縁の部分は黒色を呈している。魚の両眼は突出し、首に二つの角とひげ、頬、翅、鰭がすべてそろい、全身は鱗文で飾られ、尾部は曲折し、下方に波浪が描かれ、あたかも水中からおどり出す姿を示す。魚の開いた口を瓶の口とし、腹部に小龍一つがある。玉自体の色彩を利用して巧みに彫刻したもので、こうしたものを通称して「巧作」という。

26　清　白玉茶壺

高さ 10.7cm　縦 10.25cm　横 16.8cm

　口のしまったまるい水さし形の壺である。壁は厚く高台は低く、水さし口と把手がある。全体に光沢があり、飾り模様はない。口は鳳首の形をしており、把手は如意の形である。蓋の表も光沢があり、上に蓮の花を施してある。底には隷書で「嘉慶御用」の四字がある。色は青みがかった白色を呈し、玉質はつややかで光沢があり美しい。

27　清　白玉四耳彝炉

高さ12.8cm　縦 15.4cm　横 17.1cm

　円形で、口が大きく、壁は短く、腹部はやや広く、底は浅くくぼみ、装飾的な四つ足をもつ。耳は四龍の形に刻まれ、それぞれに一つずつ活環がついている。蓋の上に篆書で「壽」の一字があり、四つの如意耳でかこんでいる。玉質は明るくつややかで、青みがかった白色を呈する。供仏用に使われる。

28　清　白玉花薫

高さ 12.9cm　口径 13.4cm　総長 19.3cm

　円形、大口で、壁は深く、短い足をもっている。両耳に鏤空（透彫り）牡丹の浮彫りがあり、蓋を含めて全体に鏤空が刻まれ、牡丹は深彫りになっている。玉質は光沢があり、青みがかった白色を呈する。形が美しく、中に新鮮な匂い花を盛るのにふさわしい。

29　清　白玉瑞獣尊

高さ 22.1cm　縦 4.56cm　横 15.22cm

　麒麟の形をし、背に平たい角ばった瓶を負い、大口で壁は深く、腹部はやや広い。両耳は象首の形でそれぞれ活環一つを含み、首部に芭蕉葉の文様飾りがあり、腹部には雲の文様がある。獣の頂端に角が一本あり、玉の色は清らかな白色を呈している。口のまわりに隷書で「大清乾隆仿古」の六字がある。

30　清　白玉螭耳桮

高さ 5.2cm　縦 7.4cm　横 12.56cm

大口の楕円形で、壁は低く、足は短い。耳は螭形に浮彫りが一つあり、口には霊芝を含んでいる。口のまわりに蟠螭の浮彫りがあり、下方に流雲を施している。壁は光沢があり、玉質は細かくて輝きがある。螭の背には玉皮が利用されている。

31　清　青玉蓮藕洗

高さ 8.63cm　縦 3.2cm　横 30.9cm

荷（蓮の葉）、蓮、蓬心（蓮の実）の三つの形から成り、これを藕（蓮の茎）でつないで一体にし、さらに一枚の大きい蓮の葉で水を容れる洗としている。玉は輝きがあり、青みがかった白色で、形、色ともに美しい。

32　清　白玉錦茘枝

高さ 8.45cm　縦 4.83cm　横 12.31cm

錦茘枝は俗に苦瓜と呼ばれる。錦茘枝二つが一体に連なって彫られ、これを藤の葉と小さい錦茘枝一つでつないでいる。玉の色は美しい白色で、形は真に迫っている。

33　清　青玉炉

高さ 12.3cm　縦 13.5cm　耳を含めて横 18.0cm

大口の円形で、壁は低く、底はまるい。下に三本の短い足がついている。両耳に獣形があり、腹壁には獣面の文様を彫り、三本足の上端にも獣首彫りがある。蓋の頂端は透しの蟠龍に作ってある。玉質は青色。

34　清　碧玉双耳活環菊弁洗

高さ 8.3cm　口径 25.4cm　耳も含めて径 35.1cm

円形で広い口、壁は低く、底は平たく、四本の短い足がついている。全体に菊花の文様がある。菊の花弁四層に重なりあって彫られ、花蕊を中心に胡蝶が両耳に、その下にそれぞれ一つの活環がついている。底の中心部には隷書で「乾隆年製」の四字がある。

35　清　青玉天雞蓋尊

高さ 19.2cm　縦 3.72cm　横 9.12cm

器身に鳳鳥一羽を彫り、背に一瓶を負っている。口は垂直で、壁は深く、腹部はやや広い。鳳鳥は両輪の上にとまり、長い尾は内巻きになっている。これは古い銅器の天雞尊の形を模倣したものである。口のまわりに篆書で「乾隆年製」の四字がみえる。

36　清　碧玉瑚秋山猟騎図筆筒

高さ 18.1cm　径 18.2cm

　円柱形から成る。口壁は垂直で、壁が深く、底は浅くくぼんでいる。壁のまわりに浮彫りで秋山猟騎図がある。口縁の下に楷書で「秋山猟騎」の四字、また口縁にも楷書で「乾隆壬寅」(1782)の御題があり、その下に篆文で「會心不遠」の角印がある。玉の色、光沢ともによく、文飾の彫りも精細である。

　筆筒は文房器の一種で、文房四宝の一つである筆を置くのに使われる。机に置くものであるが、また優雅な飾り品にもなっている。

37　清　碧玉瑚龍三足鼎

高さ 14.4cm　口径 11.25cm　耳を含めた長さ 17.7cm

　円形から成り、広口で、壁が低く、底はまるく、下に短い三本の足がついている。両耳は龍の形で、腹壁に獣面の文様を彫り、回文文様が装飾地文になっている。三本足の上方は獅子首で下方は獣爪になっている。蓋の表にも獣面文様の彫刻があり、蓋頂に蟠龍の彫刻がある。器の裏には文様がない。玉は光沢があり、文様は精緻にできている。

38　清　碧玉鰲魚花挿

高さ 16.7cm　縦 3.6cm　横 11.0cm

　魚形で大口、壁が深く、底は浅くくぼんでいる。はねあがった大小二匹の大魚が彫られている。玉質は、光沢にみち、色は深緑を呈する。花瓶の類である。口下に篆書で「乾隆年製」の題字がある。

39　清　碧玉尊

高さ 21.6cm　縦 4.6cm　横 12.2cm

　怪獣の形をしている。獣は頭をもたげて口をあけ、勇猛な様を示す。背に瓶を一つ負い、広い口で、壁は深く、肩幅は広く、腹部はやや細い。玉は深緑を呈し、形が美しい。口の縁に篆書で「乾隆年製」の題字がある。

40　清　碧玉鏤空雲龍大香筒

高さ 77.5cm　直径 12.7cm

　円柱形から成り、中身は空で筒状になっている。全体に雲の文様が彫られ、蟠龍が一匹その上を廻っている。色は深緑色を呈する。

41　清　碧玉蟠龍洗

高さ 7.4cm　縦 9.4cm　横 13.38cm

　不規則な楕円形で、口は内部に湾曲していて、壁は深い。全体に雲の文様が

刻まれ、口縁に二匹の蟠龍の浮彫りがある。宝珠の上に楷書で「乾隆年製」の題字がある。

42　清　碧玉瑪花龍耳炉

高さ 13.2cm　縦 7.4cm　横 16.5cm

長方形から成り、口の壁は垂直で、壁は深く、底は平たく、四本の短い足をつける。蓋の表の四つの角にそれぞれ蟠龍一匹が彫られ、蓋の中央にも蟠龍がある。腹壁一面には獣面文様が刻まれ、両耳は龍で、底は光沢のある素面になっている。この彫りは精細をきわめている。

43　清　黄玉連環鈕印

中　高さ 3.81cm　縦 2.39cm　横 3.41cm
左　高さ 3.46cm　縦 2.65cm　横 2.68cm
右　高さ 3.42cm　縦 2.65cm　横 2.66cm
鎖の長さ 16.8cm

三つの印から成る。一つは楕円形、他の二つは角形で、印の上端にはそれぞれつまみがある。つまみの上には小さな鎖が一本あり、鎖の末端にある小さな環につないで一つのものとして作られている。

44　清　翠玉松鶴山子

高さ 14.0cm　縦 4.2cm　横 11.33cm

翡翠の玉を使って山岳を彫ったものである。正面の峰はまるくそびえ、石のかけ橋には泉水が流れ、高い松のかたわらには鶴と鹿を配して瑞兆の景を作っている。

45　清　翠玉白菜

長さ 18.7cm　縦 5.07cm　横 9.1cm

翡翠の玉を使って白菜を彫ったもので、玉の原色を巧みに生かしている。すなわち緑色の部分は葉に、白色の部分は茎になるように配置し、実物をよく描写している。菜の上に、きりぎりす二匹が浮彫りしてある。

46　清　翠玉松鶴挿屏

長さ 21.63cm　幅 15.4cm　厚さ 1.05cm

板状の長方形の翡翠で、一面に長寿を象徴する松鶴を、裏面には海中の蓬莱山を彫ってある。玉は翠緑色を呈し、美しい作である。

47　清　紅瑪瑙蟠桃洗

　　　　　　　　高さ 9.9cm　　縦 6.15cm　　最大の広さ 8.83cm

　樹幹の一部をとらえて彫刻され、壁は深く、底は平たい。幹のかたわらに枝
葉の浮彫りがあり、枝は屈曲して器側をめぐっている。枝には桃の実が一つ刻
まれ、口縁には純白の蝙蝠が一匹、口には霊芝を含んでいる。全体に赤色を呈
し、蝙蝠だけが白色で、赤白の対照が格別な美しさを生んでいる。

48　清　瑪瑙磨具

　　　　　　　　高さ 15.4cm　　縦 20.9cm　　横 25.9cm

　瑪瑙に彫琢を施した石臼の一組で、灰色の間に赤色がまじり、黒斑点がある。
形は円式石臼に全く近似している。

49　清　墨晶筆筒

　　　　　　　　高さ 16.6cm　　縦 8.7cm　　横 11.61cm

　黒水晶で古松の老幹を彫り、壁は深く、底は平たい。両側に枝の浮彫りがあ
り、幹には一面に松鱗を刻してある。口辺の下に草書で「松至千年能化石、此
身原不愧徂来」の題字がある。墨色の輝きを呈し、形もまた精美である。

50　清　肉形石

　　　　　　　　高さ 5.73cm　　縦 5.3cm　　横 6.6cm

　豚の肉片に似た形をした天然の石である。表面には豚の毛穴のような凹みが
散布し、皮の下には、油身と赤身があって真に迫っている。

Jade

Jade, which is a kind of stone, with its transparent body, lustrous and bright character, is defined in Shu-wen as "the fairest of stones." But jade is not the only fair stone. Agate, crystal, ruby, sapphire, lapis lazuli and turquoise are all quite beautiful. Consequently the ancients had two definitions of jade. The broad definition includes all the previously mentioned beautiful stones. The narrower definition is limited to those stones which mineralogists call jade. Mineralogists divide jade into two kinds: nephrite, the commonly seen white, blue, green, yellow, dark green, black jade. Jadeite is slightly different in colour by its bright green colour; *fei-ts'ui* is another name for jadeite to be referred to.

Jade is too hard to be cut by ordinary metals, it is very difficult to carve into objects. For thousands of years, China has always been famous for the jade carving, the tools used are very simple, while the objects are extraordinary beautiful.

The number of places referred to in Chinese old books as sources of jade are countless, they mostly meant fair stones. True jade exists in Sinkiang and Yunnan provinces, nephrite in Sinkiang and jadeite in Yunnan.

The method of carving jade was developed from carving stone. After the use of stone artifacts had become impractical, the ancients were unwilling to discard them. So they preserved them and became a memento to be worshipped. The most beautiful stone—jade—was selected as material to imitate after stone axe and stone sickle as the tallies and ceremonial jade in the court.

There are three kinds of jade objects: tallies used in the court, ceremonial jades, and ordinary jade for decoration, for inlaid work and for burial.

Among the ceremonial jade, the most important were the "liu jui" and "liu ch'i." The former was supposed to be held by people in the court as symbols of their authority: "chen-kuei" for the emperor; "huan-kuei" for a duke; "hsin-kuei" for a marquis; "kung-kuei" for an earl, these "kuei" were alike in shape, but differed in size. "ku-pi" for a viscount; "p'u-pi" for a baron, "pi" differed in decoration but were alike in shape.

"Liu ch'i" were ceremonial objects used by the emperor

in worshipping Heaven, Earth, and the Four Directions: "ts'ang-pi," greenish jade disk, used in worshipping Heaven; "huang-tsung," yellow jade cylinder, used in worshipping Earth; "ching-kuei," blue jade tablet, used in worshipping the East; "chih-chang," red jade tablet, used in worshipping the South; "pai-hu," white tiger, used in worshipping the West; and "hsüan-huang," black crescent, used in worshipping the North.

Five kinds of tallies were "chen-kuei," "yen-kuei," "yuan-kuei," "ku-kuei," and "ya-chang." They were used to console people during disaster, to subjugate an official who had committed a crime, to reward a prize to an official for his merit or good conduct, to arbitrate disputes between high officials, to marry princess, and to dispatch troops. Since early tallies were simply made and could easily be imitated, after Eastern Chou they were replaced by tiger tallies. Tiger tallies were carved in the shape of a tiger and split in two halves. One half was given to a military leader, the other half was kept by the court. When dispatched, the two halves should be fitted into one tiger, then the order is true.

Jade for ornamentation usually referred to the jade wore on the head, neck, waist, etc. The material first used were animal teeth, bird bones, etc. Later on jade took their place: "hsi," crescent shaped, derived from animal teeth worn at the waist; "lo", both round and rectangular types, derived from bones that were formerly worn at the waist; "chi," an ornamental hairpin; "kang-mao", similar in shape to square Lo, was used as a talisman against evil; "weng-chung," human-shaped talisman, etc. are all what we call pendant.

Among inlaid jade mostly referred to those inlaid in sword haft and sheath. They are "peng," "wei," "sui," and "pi." "Chang-shou" was the jade ornaments used to decorate the tops of staffs.

Funerary jades were used to insert into the nine apertures to prevent the body from decay. This is based on the belief that by doing so, the soul would be immortal. "Han," cicada-shaped jade put in the mouth of the deceased; "t'ien," inserted in the ears; and "wo," placed in the hands, are all belonged in this class.

Dancing and singing are very natural reaction when people are pleased. Dancing and musical instruments include jade axe, jade "ch'i" and jade musical stone.

In addition to those listed above, brush rest, inkstone, flower holder, flower perfumer and little trinkets are all very worthwhile to be mentioned.

Notes

1. Pei, Archaic Jade Pendent

Shang dynasty (1766–1122 B.C.)
Lengthwise: 11.35 cm.   Crosswise: 5.0 cm.   Thickness: 0.3 cm.

Bird-shaped pendent. Light brown in colour. The bird is standing with a dragon on the head.

2. Pi, Archaic Jade Plain Disc

Shang dynasty (1766–1122 B.C.)
Diameter: 37.0 cm.   Thickness: 1.36 cm.

Plain disc without decoration. Green jade with brown spots.

3. Kuei, Archaic Jade Tablet

Shang dynasty (1766–1122 B.C.)
Length: 30.6 cm.   Width: 7.2 cm.   Thickness: 1.25 cm.

Elongated flat tablet. Reddish brown in colour. One face carved with cicada pattern, the other face with bird pattern. The shape of kuei is round at the top, the inscription carved is up-side-down.

4. Kuei, Archaic Jade Tablet

Chou dynasty (1122–221 B.C.)
Length: 24.6 cm.   Width: 6.9 cm.   Thickness: 1.22 cm.

Elongated tablet with two holes, one is larger than the other. Delicated body with greyish green colour, the saturated part with brown and black colour. One face with human face decor, the other with animal face decor. With inscription on both faces.

5. Pi, Archaic Jade Disc

Chou dynasty (1122–221 B.C.)
Thickness: 0.7 cm.   Diameter: 26.4 cm.

Round disc with grain pattern on both sides. Reddish brown in colour.

6. Ts'ung, Archaic Jade Tube

Chou dynasty (1122–221 B.C.)
Height: 47.2 cm.   Crosswise: 6.73 cm.

Rectangular body with cylindrical hollow centre. Reddish brown in colour. Whole body decorated with "Ts'ung's" special decor.

7. Ts'ung, Archaic Jade Tube

Chou dynasty (1122–221 B.C.)
Height: 15.7 cm.   Crosswise: 7.0 cm.

Rectangular body with cylindrical hollow centre. Reddish black in colour. Whole body decorated with "ts'ung" special decor.

8. Huang, Archaic Jade

Chou dynasty (1122–221 B.C.)
Lengthwise: 6.0 cm.   Crosswise: 17.75 cm.   Thickness: 0.55 cm.

A tablet in the shape of half a Pi. Reddish brown in colour. Decorated with grain pattern on both sides, and with inscriptions.

9. Fu, Archaic Jade Axe

Chou dynasty (1122–221 B.C.)
Length: 12.7 cm.   Width: 5.0 cm.   Thickness: 2.45 cm.

Jade axe with a hole. With delicately carved human face on both sides. The whole body in different shade of brown colour.

10. Ch'i, Archaic Jade Axe

Chou dynasty (1122–221 B.C.)
Length: 23.1 cm.   Width: 14.0 cm.   Thickness: 0.95 cm.

Jade tablet in the shape of axe. Reddish brown in colour. Decorated with dragon pattern on both sides.

11. Huan, Archaic Jade Disc

Chou dynasty (1122–221 B.C.)
Diameter: 11.1 cm.   Thickness: 0.5 cm.

A disc with a larger orifice proportionately than that of the Pi. Decorated with grain pattern. Saturated parts with reddish brown colour.

12. Huan, Archaic Jade Disc

Chou dynasty (1122–221 B.C.)
Diameter: 17.15 cm.   Thickness: 0.4 cm.

A disc decorated with rush pattern on both sides. Greenish yellow in colour, those saturated parts with light brown colour.

13. Pi, Archaic Jade Discs (5 pieces)

Warring States period (481–221 B.C.)

Hsi pi is small disc used as pendent.

Above right: Plain disc in green colour. Saturated parts in reddish brown.
Diameter: 6.67 cm.   Thickness: 0.6 cm.

Below left: Oval disc without decoration. Green jade with light brown saturation.
Lengthwise: 6.25 cm.   Crosswise: 4.9 cm.   Thickness: 0.7 cm.

Above left: Round disc with cloud pattern decor. Green jade with dark brown saturation.
Diameter: 5.27 cm.   Thickness: 0.6 cm.

Below center: Plain disc. Green jade with light brown saturation.
Diameter: 4.42 cm.   Thickness: 0.4 cm.

Below right: Oval disc without decoration, thinner on the edge. Greenish blue jade with brown saturation.

Lengthwise: 4.2 cm.   Crosswise: 3.76 cm.   Thickness: 4.06 cm.

14. Heng, Archaic Jade Girdle Ornament

Warring States period (481–221 B.C.)
Lengthwise: 2.8 cm.   Crosswise: 20.2 cm.   Thickness: 0.55 cm.
Jade in the shape of a part of Pi. A hole on the top. With cloud pattern decor and reddish brown saturation.

15. Pi, Archaic Jade Disc

Han dynasty (206 B.C.–220 A.D.)
Diameter: 19.8 cm.   Thickness: 0.8 cm.
Jade disc with silkworm pattern decor. Greenish white jade is shinning and brownish black saturation. Inscription on both sides.

16. Yuan, Archaic Jade Disc

Han dynasty (206 B.C.–220 A.D.)
Diameter: 15.02 cm.   Thickness: 0.75 cm.
Jade disc with an orifice larger than that of the huan. Cicada pattern on one side, dragon pattern on the other side. Greenish blue in colour with brown saturation.

17. Peng, Wei, Shui, Pi. Archaic Jade Sword Ornaments

Han dynasty (206 B.C.–220 A.D.)
Above right: Peng, a sword fitting surround the mouth of the scabbard. Greenish jade with reddish brown saturation.   *Diameter: 5.1 cm.*
Below right: Wei, sword ornament with animal face and dragon pattern decor.

Lengthwise: 2.22 cm.   Crosswise: 6.53 cm.
Above left: Shui, Sword Ornament with two curl-up ends.   Decorated with two dragons on the face. With reddish brown saturated spots.

Lengthwise: 10.27 cm.   Crosswise 2.7 cm.
Below left: Pi, sword ornament with a hole on the upper part. Decorated with cloud pattern, with light brown saturation.

Lengthwise: 4.88 cm.   Crosswise: 5.72 cm.

18. Tai t'ou, Archaic Jade Belt Ring

Han dynasty (206 B.C.–220 A.D.)
Lengthwise: 6.1 cm.   Crosswise: 9.55 cm.   Thickness: 2.16 cm.
Oval rectangular jade ring suppose to engage with clothing hook. Decorated with tortoise and dragon pattern on the face. Greenish white jade with brown saturation.

19. Han, Archaic Jade Cicada (8 pieces)

Han dynasty (206 B.C.–220 A.D.)

Jade cicada is placed in the mouth of the dead.

A. Green jade with white and brown saturation.

Length: 6.11 cm.   Width: 2.97 cm.   Thickness: 0.82 cm.

B. Greenish white jade with light reddish brown saturation.

Length: 6.02 cm.   Width: 2.92 cm.   Thickness: 0.9 cm.

C. Jade with light reddish brown saturation.

Length: 6.0 cm.   Width: 3.2 cm.   Thickness: 1.23 cm.

D. Glossy white jade with brown saturation.

Length: 4.67 cm.   Width: 2.75 cm.   Thickness: 1.0 cm.

E. Jade with light brown and brownish black saturation.

Length: 6.67 cm.   Width: 3.45 cm.   Thickness: 0.67 cm.

F. Green jade with brownish black saturation.

Length: 5.03 cm.   Width: 2.55 cm.   Thickness: 0.68 cm.

G. Green jade with very light brown saturation.

Length: 5.85 cm.   Width: 2.92 cm.   Thickness: 0.5 cm.

H. Greenish white jade with dark brown saturation.

Length: 5.87 cm.   Width: 3.19 cm.   Thickness: 0.87 cm.

20. Pi hsieh, Archaic Jade Winged Beast

Han dynasty (206 B.C.–220 A.D.)

Height: 9.6 cm.   Length: 13.2 cm.   Width: 3.55 cm.

Winged beast thought to ward off evil spirit. The jade is saturated under the ground to reddish brown colour. There are inscriptions on the animal's chest.

21. Black Jade Brush Rest

Han dynasty (206 B.C.–220 A.D.)

Height: 11.5 cm.   Length: 15.7 cm.   Width 6.9 cm.

The jade is in the shape of a crouching sheep, a shepherd on the back. Black jade is lustre.

22. Handled Cup, Archaic Jade

Sung dynasty (960–1279)

Height: 12.2 cm.   Mouth diameter: 4.7 cm.

Base diameter: 3.14 cm.   Width 6.6cm.

Straight mouth, deep belly, decorated with cloud pattern on the body, and animal face pattern on the edge. Saturation appears green around mouth and light brown on the foot ring.

23. Kuang, Archaic Jade Wine Vessel

Sung dynasty (960–1279)

Height: 14.6 cm.   Lengthwise: 5.8 cm.   Crosswise: 11.79 cm.

The vessel in the shape of a dragon, with dragon head ladle. Greenish white jade with reddish brown saturation. Inscription around the mouth.

24. Hsi, White Jade Brush Washer

Ming dynasty (1368–1644)

Height: 6.0 cm.   Lengthwise: 14.3 cm.   Crosswise: 20.7 cm.

The body in the shape of a leaf, a cicada rests on the stalk, very actively and delicately carved. Greenish white jade.

25. Hua cha, White Jade Flower Holder

Ming dynasty (1368–1644)

Height: 15.6 cm.   Lengthwise: 4.26 cm.   Crosswise: 9.55 cm.

The vessel in the shape of a fish, swelling mouth, deep belly. Eyes, scales, and waves are all lively engraved. The mouth of the fish used as the mouth of the vase.

26. Cha hu, White Jade Teapot

Ch'ing dynasty (1644–1911)

Height: 10.7 cm.   Lengthwise: 10.25 cm.   Crosswise: 16.8 cm.

Round tea pot with contracting mouth, deep belly and shallow ring foot. Lotus-shaped cover. With inscription on the bottom. White jade with slightly green colour.

27. Lu, White Jade Incense Burner

Ch'ing dynasty (1644–1911)

Height: 12.8 cm.   Lengthwise: 15.4 cm.   Crosswise: 17.1 cm.

Round body, contracting mouth, shallow belly, four feet and four dragon-shaped handles. White jade with slightly green tinge.

28. Hua hsün, White Jade Flower Perfumer

Ch'ing dynasty (1644–1911)

Height: 12.9 cm.   Diameter: 13.4 cm.   Length: 19.3 cm.

Round body with contracting mouth, deep belly and ring foot. Open-worked decoration of peony cover the whole body. Sweet white jade with slightly green tinge.

29. Tsung, White Jade Wine Vessel

Ch'ing dynasty (1644–1911)

Height: 22.1 cm.   Lengthwise: 4.56 cm.   Crosswise: 15.22 cm.

The body in the shape of an unicorn, a flat vase on the back. Decorated with banana-tree leaves and cloud pattern. White jade.

30. Pei, White Jade Cup

Ch'ing dynasty (1644–1911)
Height : 5.2 cm.   Lengthwise : 7.4 cm.   Crosswise : 12.56 cm.

Oval cup with contracting mouth, shallow belly and ring foot. A serpentine-dragon with fungus in the mouth around the body. The animal is carved with the "skin" of the white jade.

31. Hsi, Green Jade Washer

Ch'ing dynasty (1644–1911)
Height : 8.63 cm.   Lengthwise : 3.2 cm.   Crosswise : 30.9 cm.

The body in the shape of a lotus leaf, lotus-root and lotus seed. White jade with green tinge. Very beautiful shape.

32. White Jade Leechee

Ch'ing dynasty (1644–1911)
Height : 8.45 cm.   Lengthwise 4.83 cm   Crosswise : 12.31 cm.

White jade two leechees, with added ivy and small leechee at the side.

33. Lu, Green Jade Incense Burner

Ch'ing dynasty (1644–1911)
Height : 12.3 cm.   Lengthwise : 13.5 cm.   Crosswise : 18.0 cm.

Round body with contracting mouth and shallow belly. Three feet. Animal-shaped handles. Decorated with animal-face pattern. Green in colour.

34. Hsi, Dark Green Jade Brush Washer

Ch'ing dynasty (1644–1911)
Height : 8.3 cm.   Diameter : 25.4 cm.   Lengthwise : 35.1 cm.

The washer is in the shape of chrysanthemum. Contracting mouth, shallow belly, flat base, butterfly-shaped handles. Inscription on the base.

35. Tsung, Green Jade Covered Vase

Ch'ing dynasty (1644–1911)
Height : 19.2 cm.   Lengthwise : 3.72 cm.   Crosswise : 9.12 cm.

Jade carved in the shape of a phoenix with a vase on the back. Straight mouth, deep belly. Imitating after bronze vase.

36. Pi tun, Dark Green Jade Brush Holder

Ch'ing dynasty (1644–1911)
Height : 18.1 cm.   Diameter : 18.2 cm.

Columnar body with straight mouth and deep belly. Decorated with "hunting in the autumn". Insctription around the edge. This brush holder is very delicately carved.

37. Ting, Dark Green Jade Cauldron

Ch'ing dynasty (1644–1911)
Height: 14.4 cm.   Diameter: 11.25 cm.   Lengthwise: 17.7 cm.

Round body with contracting mouth, shallow belly and three feet. Dragon-shaped handles. Decorated with animal face over fret pattern background. The jade is lustre.

38. Hua Ch'a, Dark Green Jade Flower Holder

Ch'ing dynasty (1644–1911)
Height: 16.7 cm.   Lengthwise: 3.6 cm.   Crosswise: 11.0 cm.

The vase is in the shape of a fish, with contracting mouth, deep belly and shallow foot. Two fishes are very lively carved in the shape of jumping. Inscription around the mouth.

39. Tsung, Dark Green Jade Wine Vessel

Ch'ing dynasty (1644–1911)
Height: 21.6 cm.   Lengthwise: 4.6 cm.   Crosswise: 12.2 cm.

The body is in the shape of a monster with a vase on the back. Contracting mouth, deep belly, and broad shoulder. Inscription around the mouth.

40. Dark Green Jade Tube

Ch'ing dynasty (1644–1911)
Height: 77.5 cm.   Diameter: 12.7 cm.

Columnar tube carved with open-worked decoration of dragon and clouds.

41. Hsi, Dark Green Jade Brush Washer

Ch'ing dynasty (1644–1911)
Height: 7.4 cm.   Lengthwise: 9.4 cm.   Crosswise: 13.38 cm.

Swelling mouth, deep belly. Carved with clouds and dragons.

42. Lu, Dark Green Jade Incense Burner

Ch'ing dynasty (1644–1911)
Height: 13.2 cm.   Lengthwise: 7.4 cm.   Crosswise: 16.5 cm.

Rectangular dark green jade burner with four feet. Decorated with coiled dragons and animal face pattern. Dragon-shaped handles. Delicately carved.

43. Yin, Yellow Jade Seals

Ch'ing dynasty (1644–1911)
Center: Height: 3.81 cm.   Lengthwise: 2.39 cm.   Crosswise: 3.41 cm.
Left: Height: 3.46 cm.   Lengthwise: 2.65 cm.   Crosswise: 2.68 cm.

Right: Height: 3.42 cm. Lengthwise: 2.65 cm. Crosswise: 2.66 cm.

Three seals joint with chains, one is oval, the other two are square.

44. Jadeite Trinket

Ch'ing dynasty (1644–1911)
Height: 14.0 cm. Lengthwise: 4.2 cm. Crosswise: 11.33 cm.

Jadeite carved in scenery. Stiff, stream, pine tree, crane and deer are all very vivid decorated.

45. Jadeite Cabbage

Ch'ing dynasty (1644–1911)
Length: 18.7 cm. Crosswise: 9.1 cm. Width: 5.07 cm.

This is a piece called "technically carved composition", since it is a whole piece of jade and carved according to its natural colour into cabbage, there are two grasshoppers on the leaves.

46. Jadeite Screen.

Ch'ing dynasty (1644–1911)
Length: 21.6 cm. Width: 15.4 cm. Thickness: 1.05 cm.

Jadeite decorated with scenery. Pine tree and crane on one side, and mountains and sea on the other side.

47. Agate Brush Washer

Ch'ing dynasty (1644–1911)
Height: 9.9 cm. Lengthwise: 6.15 cm. Width: 8.8 cm.

Red agate carved in the shape of a trunk of a tree, coiled with stalk and leaves of peach tree. There is a white bate around the mouth of the vase.

48. Agate Millstone

Ch'ing dynasty (1644–1911)
Height: 15.4 cm. Lengthwise: 20.9 cm. Length: 25.9 cm.

Grey agate carved in the form of millstone, with red and black spots.

49. Black Crystal Brush Holder

Ch'ing dynasty (1644–1911)
Height: 16.6 cm. Lengthwise: 8.7 cm. Crosswise: 11.61 cm.

The body in the shape of the trunk of pine tree. Deep belly, flat base. Decorated with stalk and scale. Inscription around the mouth.

50. Meat-shaped Stone

Ch'ing dynasty (1644–1911)
Height: 5.73 cm. Lengthwise: 5.3 cm. Crosswise: 6.6 cm.

This object is carved with its natural form into a lively piece of meat.